# Accountability in Practice:

## A Guide to Professional Responsibility for Nurses in General Practice

*Dedicated to the many practice nurses I have worked with, and to my secretary Tracey Barton, without whom the work would not have been possible*

# Accountability in Practice:

## A Guide to Professional Responsibility for Nurses in General Practice

**Mark Jones**

*MSc BSc(Hons)Nurs RN RHV(Hgr Dip)*

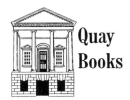

Quay
Books

Quay Books Division of Mark Allen Publishing Limited
Jesse's Farm, Snow Hill, Dinton
Salisbury, Wiltshire, SP3 5HN

British Library Cataloguing-in-Publication Data
A catalogue record is available for this book

© Mark Allen Publishing Limited, 1996
ISBN 1 85642 152 X ✓

Printed in the UK by Butler & Tanner Limited, Frome and London

# Contents

## Part I

**Preface**                                                                vii
**Chapter 1:**    Lessons from History                                       1
**Chapter 2:**    Accountability in Practice                                 17
**Chapter 3:**    Settings the Standards — The UKCC Professional            25
                  Framework
**Chapter 4:**    When Things Go Wrong — Regulating the Profession          43
**Chapter 5:**    Accountability in a Legal Context                         53
**Chapter 6:**    Accountability in an Employment Context                   61

## Part II

**Case Studies:**    Introduction                                          69
**Case Study 1:**    Practice Nurse Mary Ellis                             71
**Case Study 2:**    Practice Nurse Millie Gordon                          75
**Case Study 3:**    Practice Nurse Katy Marsh                             79
**Case Study 4:**    Practice Nurses Sue Garth, Beth Willis, Meg Brooks    83
                     and Lynn Taylor
**Case Study 5:**    Practice Nurse Susan Moor                             89
**Case Study 6:**    Practice Nurse Alicia Denton                          95
**Case Study 7:**    Practice Nurse Victoria Swan                          101
**Case Study 8:**    Practice Nurse Carol Teale                            107
**Case Study 9:**    Practice Nurse Irene Neil                             111
**Case Study 10:**   Practice Nurse Carol Moor                             115
**Case Study 11:**   Practice Nurse Erica Bligh                            119
**Case Study 12:**   Practice Nurses Amanda Taylor and Alison Richards     125
**Case Study 13:**   Practice Nurse Maria Forster                          129
**Case Study 14:**   Practice Nurse Nerys Davies                           133
**Case Study 15:**   Practice Nurse Lisa Turner                            137
**Case Study 16:**   Practice Nurse Totty Maize                            143

# Preface

Even though practice nursing has existed for almost 200 years, the rapid rise in the number of nurses employed in general practice since 1990 is unprecedented. With a workforce of well over 17 000 individuals, practice nursing now represents one of the major providers of primary health care in the UK.

The rapid development of practice nursing challenged many accepted precepts of nursing policy and practice in the community, not least the scope and expanded role of the nurse, the move away from direct management by senior nurses and the direct employment by general medical practitioners (GPs). These developments also created new problems. Questions concerning the competence of practice nurses to fulfil the wide-ranging roles arising in general practice, and the extent to which employment by a doctor might impinge upon the professional judgment of nurses brough a new focus to issues of accountability. This book is intended to provide an easily accessible reference point — not a massive, all-encompassing text, but a ready guide to real accountability in practice.

The book is divided into two parts. **Part I** begins with a historical overview of the development of practice nursing, highlighting some of the key developments which have had an impact on issues of professional accountability. It then moves on to consider the nature of accountability and the rules which regulate nursing practice.

At the beginning of each chapter, you will find a short list of the **Key Issues and Concepts** contained within it, and at the end there are **Action Points** which offer pointers in applying the theory you have just read to your own practice. Next you find a list of **Key Texts** which are recommended reading for more information on the subjects discussed in the chapter. These are followed by a list of **References** and, finally, each chapter finishes with a list of **Further Reading** — a general list of publications relevant to the subject area of that chapter (for ease of access, most of these are journal articles held in the Royal College of Nursing library).

**Part II** applies the theoretical content of Chapters 1–6 to the real situation of nursing in general practice. This is achieved through 16 case studies which cover the most prominent issues concerned with accountability that I have dealt with during my career at the Royal College of Nursing. Each case study draws on the real experience of a practice nurse, describing the problems faced and the solutions arrived at.

I hope that you will find this book useful, and through it become more aware of what it means to be accountable in your practice.

Mark Jones
Community Health Adviser
Royal College of Nursing

# Chapter 1
# Lessons from History

**Key Issues and Concepts:**

- **An overview of the historical development of practice nursing**
- **Practice nursing's quest for a recognised qualification**
- **The relationship between GPs and practice nurses**
- **The relationship between practice nurses other nurses, and the UKCC**
- **GPs' influence on practice nurse development**
- **The dilemma of accountability for practice nurses**

## Roots in the past

Practice nursing has a unique place within the profession and that uniqueness emanates from a most interesting history. From even a brief examination of this history we can identify the key factors which make issues of accountability of paramount importance for nurses in general practice, perhaps more so than for colleagues working elsewhere in the profession.

The position of practice nurses as direct employees has particular significance, and is rooted in history. The doctor engaged in community practice — the general practitioner (GP) — has been described as one of the oldest providers of medical care, dating back to the Apothecaries Act of 1815 (Fry, 1988). From this time the contribution of the GP's wife to the work of the practice was recognised, with the 'doctor's lady' (as she was often known) taking on the work of secretary, accountant and nurse. She was seen as the linchpin of the practice — the ultimate ancillary assistant (Lane, 1969). Haug (1976) believes that this all fitted in rather well with the attitudes and values of these early GPs, who tended to exude an air of paternalism towards their patients, with their wives/nurses being suited to the mothering role, offering care and compassion to the patient and running the occasional errand such as delivering medicines (Loudon, 1985).

Today practice nursing is still seen as a female occupation (Atkin et al, 1993), although the role of the practice nurse is somewhat different and nurses working in GP surgeries (practice nurses) are recognised as having a major role in enhancing the health of individuals and communities (Cumberlege, 1994) Practice nurses still have a unique relationship with GPs, however, in that they are the only group of nurses who are directly employed by them. This has some benefits, although it can create substantial problems, particularly with regard to accountability, autonomy and self-determination.

## A recent phenomenon

Although the role has been described in some form since the early 19th century, practice nursing is essentially a phenomenon of the last 15–20 years. An accurate assessment of practice nurse numbers is difficult to obtain, because employment by individual practices, means that detailed records have not been kept in many areas of the country, even when health authorities are reimbursing large proportions of salary costs. In addition the vast majority of practice nurses work part-time, and as statistics are produced in whole-time equivalent figures, it is hard to calculate the actual numbers of individuals in practice.

Various studies and reports indicate, however, that there has been a massive increase in their numbers from around 3 000 individuals in the early 1980s to over 17 000 today, with several key events being responsible for this exponential rise (Stilwell, 1991; Evans, 1992; Mackay, 1993; Atkin *et al*, 1993; Davies, 1994). These figures make practice nursing the fastest growing area of the nursing profession, over a period when primary health-care colleagues had little or no increase in their numbers (Central Statistical Office, 1980–1993). Between 1990 and 1994 the same studies indicated an increase in the employment of practice nurses by GPs of 200–300% depending on the geographical area; this increase was attributed to changes in the employment conditions of GPs due largely to the financial ramifications of the imposition of their new Contract in 1990, as we will discuss later.

These rapid increases in numbers have prompted many studies into practice nursing, the reasons behind the expansion, the benefits that expansion brings to patients, and particular problems that practice nurses have incurred as a result of their rapid growth.

Significantly, the numbers of community nurses, dominated by district nurses (DNs) and health visitors (HVs), remained relatively static over the same period as practice nurses experienced their meteoric rise in numbers (Central Statistical Office, 1980–1993). DNs laid claim to the delivery of care to people in their homes, whereas health visitors staked out the territory in health promotion, working with individuals, families and communities, but most specifically with women and their young children. As such, there were two main outcomes associated with the rapidly emerging practice nurses: first, the existing workforce saw a potential threat from this new branch of nursing and, secondly, the practice nurses sought to claim parity with their community nursing colleagues.

The potential threat was largely the result of role demarcation. Graham Butland, the then General Manager of Essex Family Health Services Authority (FHSA) (1991) stated:

> *In some areas there have been unseemly battles between community nurses and general practice nurses as to who puts the needle in and who takes the smears...*

Andrews (1994) also reported that HVs in particular were anxious to stress that they had had years of training and experience to reach their level of skill, whereas practice nurses with little experience were often being employed. So how did the demarcation disputes come about, and were practice nurses not qualified to do the job?

# The GP Contract

The main increase in practice nurse numbers occurred around 1990 and has been attributed to one major event, i.e. the introduction of a new Contract for GPs (Department of Health and Welsh Office, 1990). Why the new GP Contract caused such a flurry in practice nurse recruitment is summed up neatly by Pyne (1993):

> *General practice has become more sophisticated. It has become clear that even the best organised doctors cannot provide all the services which patients expect without help.*

Whether patients expected it or not, the 1990 Contract, for the first time, set GPs targets for immunisation and cervical cytology uptake, and annual review of patients aged 75 years and over, introduced new patient health checks, and required GPs to introduce health promotion sessions into their practices. Perhaps most importantly, GPs would be paid for this new health promotion work, according to whether or not they reached the targets. There was a double-edged incentive for GPs to take on practice nurses: first, to minimise their workload and, secondly, to maximise profit (Mungall, 1992), both pretty good motivators.

For example, in her survey of practice nurses for Walsall FHSA, Evans (1992) found that there had been a 300% increase in employment since the introduction of the Contract, and Davies (1994) reported that before the new Contract GPs in the South Wales valleys were actively seeking to employ new practice nurses, with a 60% increase occurring in the months before its introduction. Similarly, Robinson and colleagues (1993) found that over 50% of GPs surveyed indicated that they had taken on practice nurses and 83% had expanded the role of existing nurses to cope with the increased workload from the new Contract. The most comprehensive survey of practice nurses, Nurses Count, undertaken by researchers at the University of York in 1992 (Atkin *et al*, 1993), seemed to confirm that these local trends were indicative of a national picture, with their results indicating that most nurses (74% of the 12 437 sample) had been in their present post for less than five years, and over half for less than three years.

The clash of who sticks in the needle, does the smear or promotes health was almost inevitable then as GPs wanted to ensure that their nurses undertook this work in order that they might receive payment and reach the targets. Almost overnight, newly employed practice nurses were expected to become experts in childhood immunisations and health promotion (activities previously dominated by HVs) and the assessment of elderly people (a patient group catered for largely by DNs). As indicated by Gardener (1994), these events led to a 'dark period' in nursing history. During 1990 and 1991, the nursing press was full of articles and editorials denigrating practice nurses as 'untrained' and 'professionally naive'.

There were so many expressions of concern to the Royal College of Nursing (RCN) and the United Kingdom Central Council for Nursing, Midwifery and Health Visiting (UKCC), that practice nurses may not be competent to do this work, from practice nurses themselves and from HVs and DNs, that both organisations considered it necessary to issue impromptu guidance on these issues (UKCC, 1990a; RCN, 1990).

## The Challenge of Cumberlege

Although HVs and DNs were seemingly on the defensive so far as practice nurses were concerned, practice nurses themselves felt that they had something to prove in relation to these colleagues. Practice nursing had grown *ad hoc*, and did not have a recognised post-basic qualification, as did the other groups. The literature on practice nurse development suggests that the argument was between practice nurses and their DN and HV colleagues as to who should do what, the latter group expressing their importance by virtue of possessing post-basic qualifications, which practice nurses did not. Practice nurses were adamant that this had to change and that their contribution should be fully recognised. This quest for equality by qualification had begun some years before the introduction of the new GP Contract. The key event that brought matters to a to a head was the publication in 1986 of the report 'Neighbourhood Nursing: A Focus for Care', otherwise known as the Cumberlege Report (after the chair Julia Cumberlege).

The Cumberlege Report had many good ideas about the future of community nursing. However, these went largely unheeded by practice nurses, who found the suggestion that if the roles of HVs and DNs were augmented and made more flexible, then there would be no need for their employment by GPs, almost too much to bear. Rather than give up at the prospect of their evolution coming to a rapid end, practice nurses seemed to be galvanised into action by the Cumberlege Report. As eminent practice nurses of the time stated:

> *'Cumberlege did us a great favour. To be told we were bottom of the bucket by people who had fewer qualifications than many of us was starting to annoy us.'*

> (Ruth Cherry, nurse member of Hereford and Worcester FHSA, first practice nurse to serve on an FHSA committee; Crawford, 1991a)

and:

> *'Cumberlege was the best thing that ever happened to practice nurses, not because of what it said but because of the impact it had on us.'*

> (Meradin Peachey, Chair RCN Practice Nurse Association; Allen, 1991).

It is particularly interesting to note that while the Cumberlege Report was an England-only report, the backlash against it and what it stood for became a UK-wide phenomenon. Practice nurses had sensed, as one, the need to protect their role and claim recognition alongside their community nursing colleagues.

## The quest for recognition

Rather than see it as any form of weakness, as did others, practice nurses were keen to show that they had managed to educate themselves adequately without any national recognition so far, and that such recognition was long overdue. Many practice nurses felt that they were discriminated against simply because they had not undergone a similar post-basic training to their HV and DN peers. The nursing profession reinforced this by denying practice nurses access to certain advanced practice roles. A case in point was the debate surrounding the possible introduction of prescribing rights for nurses, the suggestion being that this should be limited to only those nurses with an HV or DN qualification.

Prescribing rights for community nurses had been campaigned for by the RCN since the early 1980s, and in 1989 the Department of Health finally conceded that there may be some merit in this and commissioned Dr Judith Crown to head up a committee to investigate the possibility. The Crown Report, published in 1989, came out in favour of limited prescribing rights being conferred; however, these would initially be limited to those community nurses possessing an HV or DN qualification. Sarah Andrews (1991), who was the Director of the Queen's Nursing Institute, summarised the supposed rationale for denying practice nurses the right to prescribe as follows:

> *'I do not wish to imply that nurses other than health visitors or district nurses don't have the ability; clearly many have. At present however only those with mandatory recorded qualifications at a level beyond initial registration are those who we can be sure (or as is humanly possible) are able to undertake this responsibility.'*

Practice nurses saw this as an insult, and as evidence that they were once again being passed over because they did not have a paper qualification. The journal *Practice Nursing* championed their cause, a contemporary editorial stating the case:

> *'As every PN we have spoken to will agree, on a practical level it is ludicrous that they have been left out...It all comes back to the same old story. PNs are such a motley bunch that their qualifications and experience cannot be guaranteed in any straightforward way.'*

and:

> *'PNs won't be allowed to prescribe, and they will continue to be left behind until they have parity with DN and HV colleagues in the form of a common core educational programme. Without a qualification which says that all qualified PNs are on an equal footing with DNs and HVs, they cannot be taken seriously by the legislators, who only have qualifications to go on.*
>
> *Until their own profession recognises them, and they cease to be the poor relations of other community nurses, they will continue to be left out in the cold by the rest of the world'.*

(Crawford, 1991b)

The editorial team of *Practice Nursing* set out to prove that this was not merely rhetorical pandering to their readership by commissioning a survey to demonstrate the extent to which practice nurses were already involved in the prescribing process. The survey, produced by market researchers Martin Hamblin (1991), indicated that not only were practice nurses recommending a whole range of over-the-counter products to their patients, but they were also instrumental in influencing the prescribing decisions of the GPs for whom they worked. Many nurses were also operating under protocol arrangements with doctors, whereby they could select the most appropriate drug to give to a patient. This gave more meat to *Practice Nursing*'s case, as the journal went on the attack once again:

*'It seems that the authors of the Crown Report on nurse prescribing, and the upper echelons of the nursing profession are either extremely naive or determined to dismiss the facts. Including only district nurses and health visitors in prescribing rights is to ignore a growing number of nurses who are already prescribing.*

*Whether the UKCC, the boards, or anyone else likes it or not, PNs will continue to prescribe, and most will do it very competently and ably. However, if their profession persists in turning a blind eye to the facts, they are leaving a widening gap between what PNs are trained to do and what they actually do'.*

(Crawford, 1991b)

Practice nurses had a fair point in this regard, and the comments of the junior health minister Baroness Cumberlege to delegates attending the 1994 practice nurse annual conference in Sheffield underline the fact that there is no clarity in the arguments advanced for denying practice nurses the right to prescribe:

*'The next big step forward for community nurses will surely be the demonstration schemes (for nurse prescribing) I announced at the end of last year. I hope practice nurses will again prove themselves ready to take on new opportunities and I am looking forward to receiving their applications with a view to announcing successful sites as soon as possible'.*

What the minister forgot was that unless practice nurses had a DN or HV qualification (a minority) they would not be eligible for prescribing rights, so why should they apply to run a demonstration site? This was particularly irritating to practice nurses, given that Cumberlege then went on to praise them as key members of the community team who are:

*'...in the front-line in the drive to maintain and improve the quality in primary care — a role which has been clearly recognised by the doubling of numbers of practice nurses since 1989'*

(Cumberlege, 1994).

This duality of recognition of the work that practice nurses do, but denial of an official qualification, caused considerable consternation among practice nurses, which was generally levelled at the UKCC as the perceived guardian of the country's nursing standards.

## A recognised qualification

The general discontent reported by practice nurses following the ninth annual conference in Bournemouth in 1992 was indicative of their relationship with the UKCC. The representatives of the UKCC present at the conference maintained an intransigent and condescending tone, basically implying that practice nurses could not be awarded a recognised qualification as they had not been through a uniform process of education (Jones, 1992). Following on from this conference, many practice nurses contacted the RCN saying that they had little or no hope for their future. In a way the UKCC was in an invidious position as it had already commenced work on its Post-Registration Education and Practice Project (PREPP) (UKCC, 1990b) which was intended to chart the way forward for post-basic nurse education across the whole profession. It would have been difficult for the UKCC to address the needs of practice nurses separately, although it could have been a little more positive in its attitude.

Several reports, notably the Damant Report (1990), commissioned by the English National Board for Nursing, Midwifery and Health Visiting (ENB) in collaboration with the Boards from the three other countries of the UK, indicated that it was essential for new courses to be designed which were modular in nature, allowing access for practice nurses. The modular nature allowed nurses to gain credit for courses they had previously undertaken. The UKCC PREPP working groups picked up on this theme, and practice nurses came to pin their hopes on the outcome of their work (Dewdney, 1992).

However, hopes were dashed when the UKCC produced its consultation document on the proposals. Although it recognised the need to address practice nurses' specific problems and advocated the concept of modular courses to which they would have access, it did not recognise practice nursing as a specialty in its own right. As the details of the proposals emerged, it became apparent that practice nursing was to be included with district nursing in the category of 'nursing care of the adult' (UKCC, 1991). At the same time, educational institutions that were trying to be innovative and cater for practice nurses only made matters worse in that they were hampered by the dogmatic approach of the ENB (the agents of the UKCC responsible for educational standards). For example, Wolverhampton Polytechnic launched a modular programme in community nursing, accessible to HVs, DNs and practice nurses; however, the ENB's rules permitted only HVs and DNs to receive recordable qualifications, whereas practice nurses would receive only a certificate of attendance even though they had completed the same programme as their community nurse colleagues (Crawford, 1991b).

As with the Cumberlege Report, practice nurses did not give up when they read the UKCC's initial proposals. They mounted a campaign of action and written response to the Council, the likes of which had never been seen before. This endeavour eventually led to changes in the UKCC's final proposals (UKCC, 1994) which separated out practice nursing as a specialist branch of community nursing practice worthy of a specialist qualification. Practice nurses were jubilant, and Atie Fox (1994), who was the Chair of the RCN's Practice Nurse Association, encapsulated their feelings:

> 'This is a very positive move, it is wonderful to see that the nursing profession has finally realised that we have a specialist contribution to make'.

This ongoing struggle between practice nurses, the rest of the profession, and the guardians of public interest — the UKCC — demonstrates the difficult position of nurses in general practice with regard to identifying issues of accountability. With a profession that doubted their ability and questioned — and in some cases denied (prescribing, for example) their access to certain advancing roles — and a governing body which initially seemed reluctant to assist, how could practice nurses at grass roots level begin to work through the many questions surrounding the new and innovative work they were engaging in?

As if the position which practice nurses found themselves in with reference to the rest of the profession was not bad enough, further difficulties arose from the fact that another professional group, i.e. GPs, were not only colleagues, but also employers. This situation perhaps brought with it even greater concerns about the accountability of practice nurses.

## GPs' influence on practice nurse development

Given that the rapid growth in practice nurse numbers has been attributed to the introduction of a new GP Contract, it is not suprising that GPs have an influence on the practice nurses they employ. From the literature surveyed, this influence appears to be manifest in three main ways:

- GPs' influence on the nature of work being done by practice nurses
- GPs' influence on practice nurses access to education
- GPs' influence on practice nurse job security

### GPs influence on the nature of work done

The new Contract of 1990 set GPs targets in immunisation and cervical cytology, with financial reward attached, together with monetary incentives to introduce new health promotion programmes. This translated into practice nurses being required to work in these areas and become competent in a whole new range of activities. At the time the Contract came into being, the newly formed FHSAs (developed from the previous Family Practitioner Committees — FPCs) did not have the resources or expertise to monitor nursing activity; it appeared that so long as targets were reached and returns were sent in indicating that health promotion had taken place, then the contractual obligations of GPs were regarded as having been met. As Slaughter (1991) pointed out:

> *'This gives no incentive to the general practitioner to have better qualified nurses — for as long as targets are reached and clinic numbers attained, standards are somewhat irrelevant. With the present trend of general practitioners moving towards self-financing, their main concern is to 'balance the books' with no incentive to monitor the highest quality of available health care offered by their practice nurse'.*

This is not to say that immediately following the GP Contract, practice nurses were not up to the job, but rather that some of their employers did not consider it a priority to ensure that they were competent. Many GPs did not take this stance, although the British Medical Association (BMA) seemed to agree that the financial arrangements for the employment of practice nurses do seem to have a wide-ranging effect on the nature of the work they do, as indicated by the remarks of Malcolm Fox, chair of their General Medical Services Committee taskforce on primary care nursing:

> *'The increasingly cloudy dividing line between what is (sic) considered true nursing functions and what are delegated medical tasks needs to be reassessed.*

*We don't want to get into a position where GPs are paying out of their own pocket for nurses that are needed to provide nursing support in the community'.*

*(Practice Nursing, 1993)*

Fox's statement is not quite so bizarre as it sounds, when we consider that practice nurses' salaries are mainly reimbursed by FHSAs, generally forming some 70% of their total wage bill, these funds coming from their general medical services funding allocation. The rules of the game for payment of GPs are contained within *The Statement of Fees and Allowances Payable to General Medical Practitioners* (1990), colloquially known as the 'Red Book'. These permit such reimbursement when GPs have engaged a practice nurse to undertake 'delegated medical tasks'. Consequently, any duty which smacks of community nursing practice outside of the surgery could be seen by a GP as providing a service for which he or she is not being paid. This is a potential problem area for the practice nurse who, as the title implies, has been educated to provide a nursing service, not one consisting of delegated medical tasks. As suggested by Evans (1992), all too often the practice nurse is responsible for:

*'...the constant trade off between resources available and quality of care given'.*

and consequently:

*'The role of the practice nurse is among the most challenging and daunting in health care provision. With the increasing emphasis on primary care, the vulnerable practice nurse might well become the moral pulse of the NHS.*

*It is not all that easy, however, for practice nurses who are the employees of GPs, to keep their finger on that moral pulse'.*

Such talk of practice nurses and 'morality' obviously has a bearing on issues of accountability, particularly if such a major onus is being placed upon nurses to maintain standards at all costs.

Saunders (1991) states that:

*'Because of the new Contract there are many potential moneyspinners especially in health promotion, but if GPs don't want to do the work themselves, they may put it on the practice nurse, who may not be best placed to do it'.*

At this point we enter the debate as to whether the GP or the practice nurse should decide whether a particular activity is a nursing role and, if it is the nurse's role, whether the nurse is competent to carry it out (Mungall, 1992). This is one of the key issues in the practice nurse accountability debate.

Lamont (1994) believes that practice nurses are well able to determine their own competence, and that they should not be:

*'...hemmed in by more and more restricting rules and inflexible protocols which attempt to cover every eventuality, as with hospital colleagues'.*

Nevertheless, the guru of accountability and professional responsibility for nurses, Reg Pyne, UKCC Assistant Registrar for Standards and Ethics (now retired), insists that:

> *'The maintenance and improvement of knowledge and competence is not an optional extra but an ethical imperative'*.

> (Pyne, 1993)

Evans (1993) reminds us that practice nurses were employed by GPs to assist in their work, and suggests that their position as employee places pressure on their professional principles:

> *'In its strictures on professional accountability, the UKCC's scope for Professional Practice for nursing, midwifery, and health visiting, obliges practitioners to acknowledge limitations of competence and refuse delegated functions accordingly. The pressure on practice nurses to extend their role in order to retain their posts may put them under particular pressure to disregard this advice'*.

The point about practice nurses jeopardising their jobs is perhaps startling, and we will consider it again later. But who determines competence remains a crucial issue. Evans' concerns as to whether nurses could decline a given activity based on an assessment of their own competence is worthy of note, particularly when opinions abound such as those expressed by Dewdney (1992) the GP representative at an East Sussex consensus conference on the educational needs of practice nurses:

> *'Many aspects of practice nursing are repetitive, routine and of technical nature. Some of these skills are akin to riding a bike — once learnt never forgotten'*.

This did not sit well with the findings of Mackay (1993) that:

> *'Over the years, experienced practitioners and educationalists have expressed concern about the lack of cohesive training and development programmes for practice nurses'*.

Nor did it fit in well with Damont's belief (following the completion of her report to the ENB on practice nurse educational need) that:

> *'Most of Britain's existing 11 000 [at that time] practice nurses are expected to require further training tailored to individual needs to reach the suggested standard'*.

> (Cited in Belcher, 1991)

It is debatable whether the majority of practice nurses required additional training in the early years following the 1990 Contract, and many practice nurses would say that they did not, and that the so-called 'educationalists' did not have a clue about their work. However, the point is whether the practice nurse was free to decide this or not. The potential mismatch in GP employer and practice nurse employee due to their differing perspectives on what constitutes a competent practice nurse comes even more to the fore when we consider the role of GPs in controlling practice nurses' access to educational programmes.

## GPs' influence on practice nurse access to education

We have established that the views of GPs are likely to influence their perception of the educational needs of their employed nurses. In addition to these differences in perception, the issue of finances again raises its head (e.g. Saunders, 1991; Slaughter, 1991; Stilwell, 1991; Dewdney, 1992; Hancock, 1992; Evans, 1993; Mackay, 1993).

Given the past attitude of the UKCC, and of the nursing profession generally, to meeting the educational needs of practice nurses, it is bad enough that courses are lacking, but even more disheartening that enthusiastic practice nurses are being impeded by GP employers. As Slaughter (1991) reports:

> *'It can be very difficult to find out about relevant courses. Then, once discovered, there is the 'uphill struggle' of finding funding, time and energy to complete the course without time off from the practice'.*

Mackay (1993) affirms this position, indicating that the structure of existing courses which require nurses to attend full time, or even during the day, 'do not fit in with the demands of general practice'. The demands of general practice mean that a nurse has been employed to do a job and not to be out of the practice being educated, with the GP having to finance a replacement. Things are changing now with the increasing availability of community health care nursing courses with a general practice nursing option, but the principles of flexible access are still relevant.

Evans (1993) indicates that while GPs want a wide range of activity from their practice nurses, if the nurse they have employed is not suitably competent it is exceedingly difficult for him/her to be 'released' from the practice to make up for the deficits in her/his knowledge and ability. The reasons for these views can be identified from the comments of Elias (cited in Dewdney, 1992) expressed at the East Sussex consensus conference:

> *'Education costs time and money. Both resources must be used wisely, not wasted on irrelevant and inappropriate education'.*

Nobody can argue with such a statement, but are GPs best placed to determine what is inappropriate education for the practice nurse? While it might not have been surprising to find evidence of GPs' reluctance to allow nurses access to education, in order to minimise any potential takeover bids, the literature indicates that it is the attitude of GPs to spending or losing money which is the key determinant to allowing practice nurses access to education. Slaughter (1991) hits the nail on the head when she confirms that the reasons GPs give for not allowing their nurses to attend courses are the delay or lack of reimbursement for the cost of courses from the FHSA, and perhaps more importantly the loss of income from clinic activity which would otherwise be undertaken by the nurse. It would seem that the assertions of Stilwell (1991), even in today's new world of community nurse education, are something of a pipe dream:

> *'If practice nurses are going to be indispensable to the new world of general practice, they must get funding for proper training for the job they are going to do. This may even mean taking a year out, or working three days out of five and having the other two at College — and being paid for it'.*

## GPs' influence on practice nurse job security

It is obvious that as the employers of practice nurses, GPs are influential so far as job security is concerned. Unfortunately, as with most of what we have considered above, this is due to the financial arrangements governing the provision of general medical services. The GP Contract of 1990 used financial incentives as the means of encouraging doctors to undertake more preventive work; they could not cope and so brought in practice nurses to assist. As a bonus, the nurses generated a good deal of income under the health promotion scheme.

This income generation through health promotion illustrates admirably the way in which practice finances, and the attitude of GPs toward them, can affect practice nurses. As the health promotion scheme introduced with the new Contract became too expensive to operate (practice nurses were doing a very good job running more clinics than ever and reaching all the targets), the Secretary of State for Health, Virginia Bottomley, introduced the new system of 'health promotion banding', with payments being made at three different levels depending upon the activity of the practice. This was bad news for many GPs who had come to rely on the income from the old scheme. For example, Dr Charles Zuckerman (1992), the secretary to Birmingham Local Medical Committee, stated that:

> *'Some small practices, especially single-handed practices, who have been running a high number of health promotion clinics in order to help finance the salary of their practice nurse, might struggle to employ a practice nurse in the future'.*

He went on to confirm our earlier suspicions about the influence that GPs have on the nature of the work undertaken by practice nurses:

> *'Most practices would be seeking alternative ways to make up a shortfall and improve practice cashflow by offering more diabetes and asthma clinics (which will not be cash limited by the new proposals) and by increasing immunisations and other forms of item of service activity'.*

But will the nurses be competent to do this work, and if not will they be able to attend courses to update their skills? We turn full circle.

## Summary

Some readers may argue that I have painted a simplistic picture here and that the literature reviewed represents a historical position, even if that history is only up to five years old. I do appreciate that for every practice nurse who has had a bad deal in the practice, there are probably ten who could not say a bad thing about their employers — it's just that they don't shout about it.

It is clear that practice nurses have grown faster than any other group within the nursing profession. This growth rate has led to potential conflict with their nursing colleagues, and difficulties in defining their role, competence and educational needs have arisen both from their deviation from traditional nursing values (expressed by the UKCC) and from their direct employment by GPs. The freedom for practice nurses to determine the scope of their roles, their level of competence, and their need for education is a crucial issue. These prerequisites are essential for any practice nurse to begin to unravel the complexity of what accountability really means in practice.

As you read on, you will appreciate that there are no definitive answers to the many points raised above. All one can do is to try to identify some guiding principles which will prevent the mistakes of the past recurring in the future, and will enable practice nurses to flourish taking due regard of their professional principles. The remainder of this book sets out to do just that.

## Action Points

* *Locate yourself in the history of practice nurse development. Do you recognise any of the factors described above in your workplace?*
* *Consider whether GPs and practice nurses are simply victims of some greater political system. What are the features of that system and how can we change it?*
* *Practice nursing and general practice have formed strong bonds over the last 10 years. Who has benefited from that relationship?*
* *Do you consider practice nurses and GPs to be equals? If so, how can this relationship be strengthened, if not, how can it be achieved?*

# References

Allen M (1991) Practice Nursing profile: Meradin Peachey. *Practice Nursing* **January**: 5

Andrews S (1991) Nurse prescribing: Post-basic education, the key to expansion. *Practice Nursing* **January**: 434

Atkin K, Lunt N, Parker G, Hirst M (1993) *Nurses Count. A National Census of Practice Nurses.* Social Policy Research Unit, University of York,York:

Belcher I (1991) Facing challenges in primary health care. A report on the 1990 Primary Health Care Conference, Docklands. *Practice Nursing* **January**: 430

Butland G (1991) Practices who don't release staff for training should be hit in the pocket. *Practice Nurse* **January**: 432

Central Statistical Office (1980–1993) *Social Trends, No 14–27*. HMSO, London

Crawford M (1991a) Practice Nursing Profile: Ruth Cherry. *Practice Nursing* **October**: 4

Crawford M (1991b) PN diploma courses get the go-ahead. *Practice Nursing* **July/August**: 1

Crown J (1989) *Report of the Advisory Group on Nurse Prescribing.* Chair, Judith Crown. Department of Health, London:

Cumberlege J (1986) *Neighbourhood Nursing: A Focus for Care. Report of the Community Nursing Review.* Chair, Julia Cumberlege. (The Cumberlege Report). HMSO, London:

Cumberlege J (1994) Message to *Practice Nurse* journal readers. *Practice Nurse* **March**: 263

Damant M (1990) *Report of the Review group For Education and Training for Practice Nursing: The Challenges of Primary Health Care in the 1990s.* English National Board for Nursing, Midwifery, and Health Visiting, London

Davies G (1994) Meeting needs. *Practice Nursing* 22 March–4 April: 19

Department of Health and Welsh Office (1990) *Terms and Conditions for Doctors in General Practice. The NHS (General Medical and Pharmaceutical Services) Regulations 1974 Schedules 1–3 Amended.* HMSO, London.

Dewdney E (1992) The Search for Consensus. *Practice Nurse* **5(2)**: 79–80

Evans D (1993) Vulnerability and the Practice Nurse. *Practice Nursing* **21 September–4 October**: 11–12

Evans J (1992) PNs — A Picture. *Practice Nursing* **September**: 9

Fox A (1994) PREP Meets Needs of Practice Nurses. *Practice Nursing* **8–21 March**: 1

Fry J (1988) General Practice and Primary Health Care 1940–1980s. Nuffield Provincial Trust London

Gardener L (1994) In Search of Unity. *Practice Nursing* **8–21 March**: 12

Hamblin M (1991) Practice Nurses Research Summary. Mark Allen Publishing, London

Hancock C (1992) Quality in Education. *Practice Nursing* **May**: 41

Haug MR (1976) Issues in general practitioner authority in the National Health Service. In: Stacey M, ed. *The Sociology of the NHS.* University of Keele, Keele: 23–42

Jones M (1992) Assuring a rosy future. *Practice Nurse* **5(1)**: 7

Lamont H (1994) Unfettered by qualifications. *Practice Nurse* **15–31 March**: 300

Lane K (1969) *The Longest Art.* George Allen and Unwin, London:

Loudon ISL (1985) *Medical Care and the General Practitioner 1750–1850*. Clarendon Press, Oxford

Mackay J (1993) A tender subject. *Practice Nursing* **21 September–4 October**: 18–19

Mungall I (1992) The road to better training. *Practice Nurse* **May**: 56–61

Practice Nursing (1993) GP body decides stance on nursing (news). *Practice Nursing* **1–31 July**: 2

Pyne R (1993) Frameworks. *Practice Nursing* **21 September–4 October**: 4–15

Robinson G, Beaton S, White P (1993) Attitudes towards practice nurses — Survey of a sample of general practitioners in England and Wales. *Br J Gen Pract* **43**(366): 25–8

Royal College of Nursing (1990) *Practice Nursing — Your Questions Answered*. Royal College of Nursing, London

Saunders M (1991) Stand up for yourselves! *Practice Nursing* **January**: 20

Slaughter S (1991) *Practice Nursing* Profile: Susan Slaughter. *Practice Nursing* **November**: 2

Stilwell B (1991) Practice nurses role needs further definition. *Practice Nurse* **January:** 466

UKCC (1990a) *Statement on Practice Nurses and Aspects of the New GP Contract (1990)*. United Kingdom Central Council for Nursing, Midwifery and Health Visiting. London:

UKCC (1990b) *The Report of the Post-Registration Education and Practice Project*. United Kingdom Central Council for Nursing, Midwifery and Health Visiting, London:

UKCC (1991) *Report on the Future of Community Education and Practice*. United Kingdom Central Council for Nursing, Midwifery and Health Visiting, London

UKCC (1994) *The Future of Professional Practice — The Council's Standards for Education and Practice Following Registration*. United Kingdom Central Council for Nursing, Midwifery and Health Visiting, London:

Zuckerman C (1992) Jobs may be under threat. *Practice Nursing* **September**: 1

# Further reading

Bolden KJ, Bolden S (1986). The practice nurse: is history repeating itself? *Br Med J* **293**: 19–20

Hasler J (1992) The primary health care team: history and contractual farces. (Includes role of practice nurses in the primary health care team). *Br Med J* **305**: 232–4

Stilwell B (1991) The rise of the practice nurse. (History of practice nurses). *Nursing Times* **87**(24): 26–8

# Chapter 2
# Accountability in Practice

## Key Issues and Concepts:

- Definitions of accountability
- Accountability in relation to authority and autonomy
- To whom are we accountable?
- Accountability and the UKCC

## Some definitions

We tend to use the word 'accountability' in our everyday language, assuming that everyone knows what it means, yet the concept of accountability has been debated in dozens, if not hundreds, of articles, papers and books. As Hunt (1991) says:

*'one difficulty with accountability is that it is one of those words, like "justice", or "autonomy" which is so big almost anything can be squeezed out of it'.*

There is a consensus, though, that accountability concerns having responsibility for one's own actions, and being answerable for those actions. Let us consider these two aspects further.

Johns (1989) believes that the term 'accountability' has become distorted and vague, and that a requirement 'to be held to account' would be more meaningful. Similarly, in discussing Lewis and Batey's definition of accountability (1982), Kitson (1993) agrees that the underlying theme is being answerable for one's actions. So far as professional practice is concerned, Vaughan (1989) indicates that this notion of being answerable is a key component of that practice, defining accountability as a 'formal obligation to disclose what you have done'. The nursing profession, does of course have imposed upon it a formal obligation to be accountable, and we shall consider this later. First, we need to consider what factors play a part in whether or not an individual can be accountable, other than just an expectation that they will be responsible for their actions.

### Accountability, authority and autonomy

At a time when consideration of accountability in nursing was becoming more prevalent, the Royal College of Nursing (RCN) (1981) held a seminar to redefine the definition. This seminar came up with similar definitions to those described above, but widened the concept 'to link the degree of accountability to the degree of authority vested in the individual and stated that a nurse cannot be accountable without that authority' (Young, 1991). Lewis and Batey (1982) agree that a nurse must have the authority needed to carry out activities in such a way as to accept accountability, i.e. the nurse must have the right expertise and power to make decisions about the proper course of action in any given circumstance. Johns (1989) also identifies the need to be given the power to act as a prerequisite to accountability.

What we have then is a recognition that while nurses may be accountable for their actions, they must be given the authority to make decisions in the best interests of patients. This might include the decision not to undertake care in a particular way, or to divert resources from one area of care or patient to another in greater need. Such behaviour is represented in the term 'autonomy'. Autonomy is often used to describe a state in which practitioners, nurses or otherwise have the ability to make independent decisions about their actions; however, the term may be used more accurately to describe a state whereby individuals

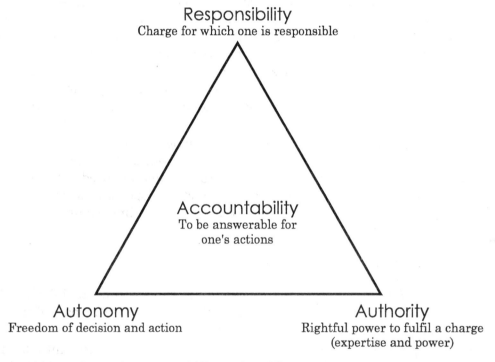

**Figure 2-1 Dimensions of accountability (after Kitson, 1993)**

are free to exercise judgment about their actions in such a way that they can truly accept responsibility for them, and consequently be held to account for those actions.

The link between accountability, authority and autonomy is an important one. The right to self-govern and to make decisions about one's practice is an essential part of being accountable. Copp (1988) sees freedom to practice according to self-determination as directly related to the principle of accountability, and Singleton and Nail (1984) reiterate that the freedom to control practice is directly correlated with the responsibility taken in initiating nursing action. This is also important for professional development, as nurses who are constrained in a system whereby they are unable to exercise sufficient discretion within it in order to achieve personal goals can easily become frustrated. In such a system, innovation can be stifled as there is little room to grow.

In order to consider accountability in this way, Johns (1989) proposes that two aspects of autonomy are required: **structural** autonomy and **attitudinal** autonomy. Structural autonomy defines what is actually expected of the nurse in any given situation; this would generally be summarised in the job description. Attitudinal autonomy is the attitude of mind which says that 'I have the power and ability to practise in such and such a way, I am responsible for deciding how I practise, and I am accountable for that practice'. Johns believes that the notion of attitudinal autonomy was particularly relevant in the early days of practice nursing. As shown in the brief history earlier, practice nursing grew from a situation where GPs wanted their own nurses to whom they could delegate aspects of their work, first because they often had to engage in lengthy negotiations with nurse managers if they wanted health authority-employed staff to help and, secondly, because of the sheer workload involved in providing care to a practice population. Johns highlights the relationship between the GP employer seeing the practice nurse as a 'handmaiden', and the ease with which some nurses seemed to accept this role, as being counterproductive to autonomous nursing practice and affecting the ability of practice nurses to be truly accountable for their actions.

This situation is obviously changing in general practice, as practice nurses affirm their position as equal partners with their GP colleagues. However, as Hunt (1991) asserts, when the profession seeks to define more clearly its role, skills, knowledge base, aims and research objectives, and to identify specific and distinctive responsibilities which belong to it and nobody else, issues of accountability become even more important.

## Accountable to whom?

We have considered the definition of accountability with its prerequisite links to authority and autonomy, and acknowledged that to be accountable is an essential part of the nurse's duty as a professional. But who are nurses accountable to?

As individuals claiming to be professional care-givers, nurses are accountable first and foremost to the patients they give that care to; secondly, they are accountable for their actions as members of the nursing profession; thirdly, they are accountable to the employer; and finally, they are accountable to themselves. We can look more closely at each of these tracks of accountability, none of which can really exist in isolation.

### Accountability to patients

As with any other professional group setting out to give care to patients, nurses are directly responsible for the level of service they provide. At the simplest level, the public is right to expect a high quality of care from a nurse, and the nurse is bound to deliver care to that standard. Generally speaking, this level of care is determined informally as a result of patient–nurse interaction and some common acceptance of what nursing is about. That is to say patients rarely enter a GP surgery with a list of standard statements to be presented to the practice nurse before they allow that nurse to undertake a particular activity; rather, they rely on the general information about the practice nurse which may be presented in the practice leaflet, or may have been passed on from other patients. Patients also rely on the fact that the nursing profession itself is responsible for ensuring high standards among its members.

This seemingly 'cosy' relationship can go awry, however, should the patients (or their representatives) feel that they have not received care of a high enough standard. In order to seek redress, patients have several choices: they can ask the nursing profession to investigate the seemingly low standard of care; they can seek an explanation or redress from the GP employing the nurse; they can complain to the health authority responsible for standards of care in their area; or they can ask the representative of the community at large, i.e. a court of law, to investigate that standard, with the possible award of financial recompense should that level of care be found wanting.

The issue of accountability in a legal context is considered in more detail in Chapter 5.

## Accountability to the profession — the UKCC

Should the patient choose to ask the practice nurse's own profession to make a judgment about the standard of care he/she has received, and that nurse's ability to deliver care to a sufficiently high standard, then that decision would result in an approach to the governing body for the profession — the United Kingdom Central Council for Nursing, Midwifery, and Health Visiting (UKCC), often referred to as the Council.

Practice nurses have had many recent dealings with the UKCC, not least concerning their desire to have a specialist qualification recorded on the professional register, and it is worthwhile considering the response to this issue in particular in order to identify the reason for being of that body.

Practice nurses bombarded the UKCC with requests for recognition, but it was only when those requests began to be couched in terms which reflected the need to be able to identify a given standard of service under the professional specialism of 'practice nursing' that things began to happen. Although all registered nurses pay a periodic fee to the UKCC in order to maintain an effective registration, the prime objective of the Council is not to fight for nurses' rights, but rather to protect the interests of the public. This may not seem fair, but it is essential to separate the notion of a body which represents nursing interests, such as a trade union or professional organisation, from one which was established in order to maintain satisfactory standards of practice. Of course the UKCC has an interest in promoting and developing the art and science of nursing, but it exists first and foremost to ensure that nurses are accountable to the public for their actions.

## The UKCC remit

You will have heard of the UKCC referred to as the 'statutory body' for nursing. This definition arises from the fact that the creation of the UKCC is founded in the law of the land, i.e. in statute. The Nurses, Midwives and Health Visitors Act 1979 laid the foundations for the UKCC and, as Pyne (1992) indicates, identified two central requirements of the Council:

> *'The principal functions of the Central Council shall be to establish and improve standards of training and professional conduct.'*

and:

> *'The powers of the Council shall include that of providing, in such a manner as it thinks fit, advice for nurses, midwives and health visitors on standards of professional conduct.'*

As well as these two key responsibilities, the Act provides the Council with the ultimate power for maintaining professional standards in that it is charged to:

> *'Make statutory rules (that is, to prepare subordinate law for approval by senior Government law officers) governing the circumstances and and the means by which a person's name may be removed from the register.'*

(UKCC, 1990)

Although all of this might seem rather daunting, it was good news for the nursing profession that the 1979 Act permitted the Council to determine the method for its regulation in this way. As Kitson (1993) indicates, it is far better to have a situation whereby nursing can regulate itself internally than to have the old external regulatory mechanism as embodied in the General Nursing Council. Pembrey (1989) believes that nursing was only becoming mature enough at the time of the Act, and that before this it would have been difficult to argue for and develop an effective form of self-regulation for the profession, as nursing was constrained by such factors as a powerful management hierarchy, poor training, lack of individual autonomy, paucity of nursing knowledge, and a dominant culture of 'getting by'.

## Summary

The formulation of the Nurses, Midwives and Health Visitors Act 1979 and the beginnings of the UKCC were indicative of the nursing profession coming of age. Kitson (1993) sees these developments as representative of the nursing profession passing through a transitional phase towards a profession that is characterised by a less dominant hierarchy, ongoing education, a focus on research and development, and an emphasis on personal accountability — all hallmarks of a true profession.

The Council was permitted to establish a mechanism of self-regulation with the ability to judge standards of practice — a key attribute of any profession. But how did it set about this task and how does it fulfil these obligations today? Chapter 3 discusses the standards and guidance used by the UKCC in order that nurses may be held to account by the profession — primarily the *Code of Professional Conduct* (UKCC, 1992a) and *The Scope of Professional Practice* (UKCC, 1992b). Chapter 4 goes on to consider the system employed by the UKCC once an allegation has been made concerning a nurse's practice which may lead to a verdict of professional misconduct.

## Action points

* *What does being accountable mean to you?*
* *Do you have the authority and autonomy to be truly accountable?*
* *Why is the UKCC able to call you to account?*
* *Should nurses always be held to account for their practice?*

# Key Texts

Pyne RH (1992) *Professional Conduct and Discipline in Nursing, Midwifery and Health Visiting.* Blackwell Scientific Publications, London:

UKCC (1996) *Ethical Guidelines for Professional Practice.* UKCC, London:

# References

Copp G (1988) Professional accountability: the conflict. *Nursing Times and Nursing Mirror* **84**(43): 42–4

Hunt G (1991) Professional accountability. *Nursing Standard* **6**(4): 49–50

Johns C (1989) Accountability and the practice nurse. *Practice Nurse* **2**(7): 303–4

Kitson A (1993) Accountable for quality. *Nursing Standard* **8**(1): 4–6

Lewis F, Batey M (1982) Clarifying autonomy and accountability in nursing service, Parts 1 and 2. *J Nurs Admin* **XII**(9): 10–15

Pembrey S (1989) The Development of Nursing Practice: A New Contribution Inaugural lecture. Launch of new National Institute for Nursing. Green College Oxford.

Pyne R (1992) The Code of Conduct. (UKCC Code of Conduct's guidance on accountability). *Practice Nursing* **January/August**: 12

Royal College of Nursing (1981) *Accountability in Nursing.* RCN Seminar. RCN, London:

Singleton EK, Nail FC (1984) Autonomy in nursing. *Nursing Forum* **11**: 123–30

UKCC (1990) *'...with a view to removal from the register...'? An Explanation of the System for Considering Complaints Against Registered Nurses, Midwives and Health Visitors which Call into Question their Appropriateness to Practice.* UKCC, London

UKCC (1992a) *The Code of Professional Conduct.* UKCC, London

UKCC (1992b) *The Scope of Professional Practice.* UKCC, London

Vaughan B (1989) Autonomy and accountability. *Nursing Times and Nursing Mirror* **85**: 54–5

Young AP (1991) *Law and Professional Conduct in Nursing.* Scutari Press, London: 37

# Further reading:

Carlisle D (1990) Are you accountable? (Accountability and the UKCC Code of Professional Conduct) *Nursing Times* **86**(21): 26–9

Chappell A (1985) Accountability: the exercise of power. *Highway* **1**(3): 4–6

Devine J (1990) Exercise your rights, (UKCC's policy document 'Exercising accountability'). *Nursing Times* **86**(21): 301

Lindhoj A (1985) Accountability — the commitment to trust. *Highway* **1**(2): 4–7, 14

McSweeney P (1990) Accountability in nursing practice. (Advocacy and accountability) *Nursing Standard* **4**(24): 30–1

Norton J (1991) Accountability and the practice nurse. *Practice Nursing* Feb: 5–6

Oliver G (1988) Accountability in nursing. *Nursing Standard* **29**(2): *Advances in Clinical Practice Supplement*: 8–19

Silver JI (1986) Professionalism/autonomy. (And accountability – a bibliography). *J Nurs Admin* **16**(1): 43

# Chapter 3
# Setting the Standards — The UKCC Professional Framework

## Key Issues and Concepts

- An overview of The Code of Professional Conduct
- Consideration of the intent of the Code
- How the Code applies in everyday life and practice
- An overview of The Scope of Professional Practice
- Application of the Scope guidelines to everyday practice

## The UKCC *Code of Professional Conduct*

The *Code of Professional Conduct* first appeared on 1 July 1983 and is currently in its third edition — published in June 1992 (UKCC, 1992a). Reg Pyne, UKCC Assistant Registrar for Standards and Ethics (now retired), who could probably be described as the 'father' of the *Code of Professional Conduct*, describes it as a 'portrait' of the kind of practitioner the Council wants to see, and identifies three main reasons for it being produced:

- To establish more clearly the extent of accountability of nurses on the register
- To assist practitioners in exercising accountability to achieve high standards of practice
- To encourage practitioners to assert themselves in the best interests of patients

(Pyne, 1992a)

Similarly, in its most recent publication concerning the *Code*, the UKCC indicates that it sets out:

- The value of registered practitioners;
- Your responsibility to represent and protect the interests of patients and clients;
- What we expect from you and
- To whom you must answer

(*Ethical Guidelines for Professional Practice* UKCC 1996, Section 3)

The *Code* is essentially the 16 'commandments' of professional nursing practice, and really should take pride of place on the bookshelf or in the desk drawer of all practice nurses. It takes no more than five minutes to read through the *Code*, and an understanding and appreciation of the intent of this small but powerful document will help you come to terms with the vast majority of problems you might face in your work. In the words of Pyne (1992b):

> *'By examining two or three clauses together, for example, those concerned with maintaining and improving your competence, acknowledging your limitations, confidentiality and the environment of care, a picture emerges of nurses who will not silently accept the intolerable. Instead they will articulate in their representation about things which obstruct delivery of good care, and will expose those things which jeopardise standards, place patients at risk, or abuse colleagues.'*

Let us move on to examine the *Code of Professional Conduct* in more detail, and consider why its original architect held it in such regard.

## Your contract with the profession — four guiding principles

As you open your copy of the *Code* (which you have obtained free from the UKCC), you will notice first an introductory paragraph which states that:

> *'Each registered nurse, midwife and health visitor shall act, at all times, in such a manner as to:*
> * *safeguard and promote the interests of patients and clients;*
> * *serve the interests of society;*
> * *justify public trust and confidence and*
> * *uphold and enhance the good reputation of the professions.'*

These introductory words essentially form your contract with the profession, they are unequivocal, and set the standard to which you must aspire in order to call yourself a nurse, and be registered as one. The first sentence is dramatic in itself: we are required to act in the way described 'at all times', not just when we are at work, in uniform or on the way to work, but at **all** times. This places a great responsibility on nurses to act in a way befitting the profession in all aspects of their lives; there is perhaps no other profession which makes such a requirement or, if it does, documents it so explicitly.

Indeed nurses have been struck off the professional register by virtue of acts which on the face of it have no relevance to their nursing practice. For example, the *Daily Mail* of 3 August 1991 reported:

### Brake on Nurse

*A STAFF nurse who repeatedly took to the road despite failing six driving tests was struck off for misconduct yesterday. Valerie Dennis, 38, of Knutsford, Cheshire, built up a string of motoring convictions, a professional conduct committee in Manchester heard. Later she still hoped to pass her test.*

It is true that not many nurses have been removed from the register for driving offences such as these, but let us consider why the conduct committee reached such a decision. Clearly Ms Dennis' actions in no way jeopardised the interests of her particular patients (unless of course she had run them over while being an uninsured learner driver). However, there could be some doubt about the broad interpretation of her needing to 'serve the interests of society'. Her actions may well have undermined 'public trust and confidence in the profession' and she would have been seen as putting a definite dint in 'the good standing and reputation of the professions', something which her actions did not exactly 'uphold'.

You might consider this to be unfair, and believe that the UKCC should have better things to do than judge nurses on the standard of their behaviour outside of the work environment. Perhaps it is just unfortunate that nursing has an image which personifies good, clean-living individuals — 'angels' if you like — and when a nurse sets a foot wrong the attention of the media is more sharply focused than if it were some other member of society. We see images of nurses used every day to sell and endorse products, not only in trade journals, but also in local newspapers to sell houses, and in magazines to advertise a wide variety of products. Nursing is an image which appeals, and it is to this standard that the UKCC has to judge when applying its *Code of Professional Conduct*.

None of you would argue that the UKCC is right to use the four guiding principles when measuring the personal characteristics and actions of nurses in the context of their professional practice. This is the prime focus of the 16 clauses of the *Code*.

## The 'Stem' sentence

Following on from the statement of the four guiding principles, the *Code* contains a stem sentence, preceding all 16 of its clauses:

> *'As a registered nurse, midwife or health visitor, you are personally accountable for your practice and, in the exercise of your professional accountability, must:'*

Note the word 'must'. As Pyne (1994) says, 'accountability is not an optional extra', and the UKCC requires nurses, practice nurses included, to adhere to all 16 clauses of the code. This stem sentence also emphasises **personal accountability**: the UKCC will not accept anyone else being accountable on your behalf — not a practice manager, a nurse colleague, an FHSA nurse adviser, or a GP — only you can carry the accountability for your practice. Bear this in mind as we continue through the main body of the *Code*.

## The 'brass plaque' clause

I am often asked which is the most important clause of the *Code*, and not surprisingly the answer is the first one. If you can only commit one clause to memory, let clause 1 be that which is emblazoned on an imaginary brass plaque on your treatment room wall. It reads:

> *'...act always in such a manner as to promote and safeguard the interests and well-being of patients and clients;'*

A simple statement really, but if at any time you have the faintest doubt in your mind that what you are doing or about to do for a patient does not fit with this statement, than you should not be doing it. There is no point scanning through the remaining 15 clauses for some way of justifying your practice; if you cannot put your hand on you heart and acknowledge clause 1, then your practice is wanting in some way.

## Acts or omissions

So far we have considered accountability in the context of your actions as a professional nurse. The *Code of Professional Conduct* does, however, draw our attention to the need to have regard for 'omissions also'. This is acknowledged in clause 2, which elaborates on the same theme as clause 1. It reads:

> '...ensure that no action or omission on your part, or within your sphere of responsibility, is detrimental to the interests, condition and safety of patients and clients;'

Making sure that **you** do not do anything or miss anything out which might cause a patient to come to harm seems straightforward enough, but this clause also takes us into the territory of potential responsibility for the actions or omissions of others. No-one has fully defined what an individual nurse's 'sphere of responsibility' is, and given the diversity of practice and roles it would be difficult to do so. This is where our earlier consideration of accountability linked with authority and autonomy becomes particularly relevant.

Clause 2 ensures that those responsible for other nurses, i.e. nurse managers, are clear that if their actions or omissions cause those for whom they are responsible to jeopardise standards of practice, then they may be called to account. A practice nurse who has, as part of her job description, the responsibility to supervise a junior nurse, and abdicates that responsibility, could be called to account for any error that nurse makes, this clearly being within her sphere of responsibility.

Both the opening clauses of the *Code* leave no doubt in anyone's mind that its intention is to meet the needs and serve the interests of the public, i.e. our patients. The remaining 14 clauses advise as to how this aim is to be achieved, and can generally be grouped into five categories:

- being sure of one's competence to practise (clauses 3 and 4)
- working as a partner with patients and their families (clauses 5, 7 and 10)
- ensuring a safe and caring environment (clauses 11, 12 and 13)
- working as a team member (6 and 14)
- the need for integrity (8, 9, 15 and 16).

## Competence to practice

Bearing in mind that we have already established that the key roles of the UKCC are to ensure high standards of care and protect public interest, it is not suprising that the *Code* should emphasise the need for nurses to be adequately prepared for whatever activities they are expected to undertake in their practice. Clause 3 states quite simply that you must:

> '...maintain and improve your professional knowledge and competence;'

This speaks for itself, in that it is entirely reasonable to expect a professional nurse to take appropriate steps to keep up to date with current trends in practice, and so maintain a high level of competence. It is worth noting that this assumption has been present in all editions of the *Code*, right back to 1983, and that the recently introduced requirements of the UKCC for nurses to demonstrate ongoing learning so as to maintain their status as registered practitioners simply build on this statement and should not come as a suprise to nurses and their employers. Employers of nurses should also bear in mind their responsibility for assisting them in maintaining and updating their knowledge base.

Practice nurses working in isolation should take specific note of clause 3, and ensure that they are able to test their level of competence with colleagues, either through a formal programme of periodic refreshment, if possible, or at least through an informal network. Over time I have dealt with practice nurses who are 'conscious incompetents', i.e. they know that their skills are lacking but try to make amends. They are bad enough in respect of their *Code of Professional Conduct*, but at least they know their limitations. The most dangerous nurses I have come across are the 'unconscious incompetents', i.e. those who have no idea that their practice is substandard. It is in the interests of both patients and all practice nurses that membership of both of these groups — particularly the last — is phased out as soon as possible.

Clause 4 gives further guidance on what nurses should do if, having taken notice of clause 3, they decide that they are not competent to perform a particular activity required of them to a sufficiently high standard. Clause 4 states that you must:

> '...acknowledge any limitations in your knowledge and decline any duties or
> responsibilities unless able to perform them in a safe and skilled manner;'

This might sound to be just as much common sense as clause 3; however, from experience in giving advice to RCN members, this does not appear to be quite so straightforward. As our introductory history indicated, there appear to be some problems around differing perceptions on the part of practice nurses and GP employers as to what makes a competent practitioner. Case study 4 (page 83) specifically addresses this point. Suffice to say, whatever the pressures you might experience in your practice, if you believe you are not competent to do something, remember the 'brass plaque' clause and either do not start it or stop doing it. The discussion of the case study gives further guidance on this.

## Partnership with patients and their families

Through the *Code* the UKCC reminds us that nursing is not just about giving care to the patient we are attending, but that in practising what we call and know as holistic care, we must also encompass their relatives and family. The UKCC has not quite adopted the full spectrum of 'politically correct' terminology, but we can assume that the term 'families' applies to anyone who is significant to the life of the patient concerned.

Clause 6 explains how nurses should:

> '...work in an open and co-operative manner with patients, clients and their
> families, foster their independence and recognise and respect their involvement in
> the planning and delivery of care;'

Again, this is a clause which initially seems reasonably straightforward, yet its implementation may need some thought. Consider, for example, the situation where relatives do not want the patient to know what the diagnosis really is — usually in the case of terminal illness. The argument put forward in defence of this is something like 'it is in his best interests' or 'he wouldn't want to know'. In such a situation the nurse has to make a judgment in balancing the families' wishes with what is best for the patient. Working cooperatively with the family, perhaps discussing why it might be better for the patient to know exactly what is happening in some cases, will help to resolve the dilemma. We must not forget the 'brass plaque' clause which precedes all the others, i.e. act always in the best interests of the patient. Unfortunately, there are no hard and fast guidelines as to how we do this — it is for the nurse to decide, in discussion with colleagues, relatives and family members. (See UKCC 1996 Ethical Guidelines for Professional Practice, sections 20–25 for further discussion of these issues).

This clause also has implications in the reverse situation when a patient may not want family or friends to know details of their care. This could be so in the case of a minor who is receiving family planning advice and specifically requests that her family is not told the details of her situation. Case study 5 (page 89) discusses this scenario in more detail. Once more, in discussion with the patient and consideration of all eventualities, the nurse has to make a decision as to how far associates of the patient should be involved in their care, while putting the best interests of that patient first.

Clause 7 also requests that we consider the patient or client as an equal partner, in that we respect their particular qualities and work to deliver appropriate care irrespective of their value system or beliefs. Nurses must:

> '...recognise and respect the uniqueness and dignity of each patient and client, and respond to their need for care, irrespective of their ethnic origin, religious beliefs, personal attributes, the nature of their health problems or any other factor;'

This clause reminds us that nursing has no place for prejudice or discriminatory action, and that nurses who have strong feelings about certain groups of patients which might impede their ability to care for them should either take urgent steps to achieve a change in attitude or consider alternative work. Sadly, I can recall many cases of nurses requesting advice from the RCN concerning the care of patients with certain diagnoses, notably human immunodeficiency virus (HIV) infection, essentially looking for a 'let out' from caring from them. Fortunately the majority of such requests were motivated by ignorance, and provision of facts concerning their patients brought about attitudinal change. Think carefully about your own prejudices, if you have any, and take steps to ensure that they will not affect the way you give care.

Clause 8 gives nurses the only real option to voice concern that they may not be able to deliver a satisfactory standard of care to a patient because of their own beliefs, indicating that those who find themselves in such a position must:

> '...report to an appropriate person or authority, at the earliest possible time, any conscientious objection which may be relevant to your professional practice;'

This clause does not provide absolution from clause 7, but rather it provides a means whereby nurses with legitimate reasons for opting out of a particular caring scenario may do so. The classic example is the nurse who has strong religious beliefs leading to the inability to accept reasons for termination of pregnancy. Other situations might involve a nurse who has personal experience of a particular problem affecting a patient which might cause emotional stress. While the guidance in the clause would be appropriate here, i.e. let an appropriate person (perhaps your GP employer) know of your difficulty, this clause is not really intended for this purpose, but for true 'conscientious' objection. It is right that it is bad practice for patients to be cared for by nurses whose beliefs and emotions may jeopardise the standard of care they might give, but every nurse must balance clauses 8 and 7, and if unable to reconcile their own feelings toward patients they should obtain some guidance as to how they might overcome this difficulty.

Clause 9 continues the theme of working together with patients and respecting them as equals when giving care. It is slightly different in that it translates this respect into instructing nurses not to abuse their position by taking advantage of a person who depends upon them. Nurses must:

*'...avoid any abuse of your privileged relationship with patients and clients and of the privileged access allowed to their person, property, residence or workplace;'*

A quick reading of this clause could give the impression that the UKCC was simply looking for a polite way of saying don't 'nick' anything that belongs to a patient when you are visiting the patient at home or if you have to take the patient's property into 'safe-keeping', but it means a lot more than that.

Because nurses are registered with the UKCC and recognised as professionals, the people they care for allow them to infringe territorial boundaries in ways which would certainly be closed to others, even best friends and relatives. Although I flippantly mentioned that nurses should not steal from patients, and readers will recoil at such a suggestion, it is important to acknowledge this. More seriously, nurses and patients will inevitably be in intimate situations, and the nurse must be extremely careful not to do anything which could not be construed as part of accepted nursing practice. Because of the dependence that patients have on nurses, and the intimacy of the relationship, it is not inconceivable that emotional feelings might develop between nurse and patient. Even if a patient seemingly gives consent to a nurse becoming involved with them in a way that is not an appropriate part of their care package, the nurse should stick to the job for which she/he is there.

The UKCC is not seeking to ban romances between patients and nurses but it is stressing, in an admittedly oblique way, that nurses should not develop inappropriate relationships or undertake inappropriate actions when they are engaged in nursing practice. This does not mean a return to the old teachings of 'emotionally controlled detachment', when nursing students were tutored in the skill of 'not getting involved' and all attempts at empathy were frowned upon, but it does mean that a nurse who begins to feel strongly about a patient should take a step back and consider her position as a professional care-giver.

The final clause dealing with the nature of the relationship between nurse and patient, and the trust which should exist as partners in the caring process, is that which deals with confidentiality. Clause 10 advises that nurses must:

*'...protect all confidential information concerning patients and clients obtained in the course of professional practice and make disclosures only with consent, where*

*required by the order of a court or where you can justify disclosure in the wider public interest;'*

This clause reminds us once again that we have a privileged relationship with patients. Patients will tell you things about themselves which they would never dream of telling anyone else, other than perhaps their doctor. It is important that you give some thought as to how you might deal with issues of confidentiality in your practice before any complications arise. Remember that the clause does not only apply to information which patients say they want to give you in confidence, but indicates that all information gained in the course of your practice is potentially confidential. Of course, if a patient specifically says he/she want to tell you something in confidence, then this should be particularly respected. Consider, though, how you might react to such a statement. If you agree to this, could you be prevented from obtaining additional care for the patient by being unable to consult with a colleague without his/her express permission? On the other hand, if you tell a patient that you are not willing to accept what is said in strict confidence, but might have to share it among your team colleagues in order to provide the best care, will this prevent the patient from disclosing his/her needs?

Consider also the situation where a GP colleague (your employer) makes what could be seen as a reasonable request for you to provide details of all the patients you have discussed a particular problem with. To what extent do you protect the confidentiality of your nursing notes? If, as is often the case, the practice uses joint nursing and medical records, computerised or otherwise, what say do you have as to the confidentiality of entries you have made? There are no straight answers to these questions, and you will have to make a decision based on the merits of each case; it is wise to discuss possible scenarios with your practice team before the event arises. Case study 5 (page 89) is a classic example of what not to do.

The exemption parts of clause 10 are worth considering. No matter how unacceptable it might seem from a professional standpoint, if you are required to provide patient information by a court order, you have little choice, although you would be wise to discuss this with the rest of your team and perhaps your professional organisation. The second exemption, that of 'the wider public interest' is more difficult. Case study 15 (page 137) describes a situation in which a practice nurse had to decide what was in the public interest, and through it I have tried to explain the decision-making process you will have to go through in such a situation. Again, it is best to consider your possible reactions in such a situation, before that situation arises. (See UKCC, 1996: Ethical Guidelines for Professional Practice sections 62–73 for further discussion of confidentiality)

**Ensuring a caring environment**

Clauses 11, 12 and 13 describe the consideration you must give to the environment in which care is provided, and what you must do if you believe that environment to be unsatisfactory. Clause 11 advises that you must:

'*...report to an appropriate person or authority, having regard to the physical, psychological and social effects on patients and clients, any circumstances in the environment of care which could jeopardise standards of practice;*'

and clause 12, that you must:

'*...report to an appropriate person or authority any circumstances in which safe and appropriate care for patients and clients cannot be provided;*'

Taken together, these clauses form a powerful tool for ensuring the optimum environment of care. The practice nurse who rang me to ask what she could do to stop her and her patients being disturbed by the receptionist who kept knocking the screens to one side as she tried to get to the filing cabinets in the back of the treatment room, obviously needed to turn to these clauses in order to start building her case for a radical rethink in the geography of the practice. Similarly, practice nurses who tell me they have to take a patient along a corridor trying to find a consulting room which has been vacated by a GP out on house calls could use these clauses.

Clauses 12 and 13 refer not only to the built environment, but also to equipment. The practice nurse in case study 10 (page 115) who only had three specula with which to conduct a full cervical smear clinic would have been able to use these clauses to make her point. But who do you make the point to? Who is the 'appropriate person or authority'? This will depend on the circumstances in your practice, and who has responsibility for the area in which there is a problem. Many larger practices delegate responsibility for health and safety issues to the practice manager, for instance, and the same person might be responsible for repairs and buying new equipment. If the senior partner has ultimate responsibility for the practice, then they are the responsible person. In the unfortunate circumstance that you have presented a logical case using clauses 11 and 12, and those responsible refuse to act, then you should consider other options, such as informing the health authority responsible for the area in which your practice is located. This should only be a last resort, after all other options have failed, but remember the 'brass plaque' clause: if you were to continue to practise in an environment which you have identified as not being appropriate to high standards of care delivery, are you acting in the best interests of patients?

A final point on these clauses concerns workload. The interpretation of clause 12 would include a situation where the nurse felt that the volume of work was such that a satisfactory standard of care could not be provided. The nurse in case study 3 (page no 79) could have used this clause to prevent the tragic situation the study describes. Again, you must consider the interests of your patients: it might be acceptable for the odd patient to be squeezed into your busy appointment list, but if this happens regularly and you know that you are rushing, should you not do something about it?

Clauses 11 and 12 are not intended to provide you with the wherewithal to argue for a palatial office and treatment room with every conceivable up-to-date piece of equipment, to be used by yourself and your massive team of colleagues. However, they have been used successfully by many practice nurses to make a stand for a satisfactory caring environment, often when, through oversight rather than deliberate neglect, things have not been quite as they should.

## Teamwork

The discussion around several of the clauses above emphasises the need to work as part of a team so as to ensure high standards of care delivery. Clauses 6 and 14 particularly refer to this aspect of professional responsibility.

Clause 6 states that nurses must:

*'...work in a collaborative manner with health care professionals and others involved in providing care, and recognise and respect their particular contributions within the care team;'*

There is not much more to be said about this, other than to emphasise the need for collaboration. All team members will bring differing abilities to the care of a patient, and these need to be brought together in a comprehensive package of care, rather than being delivered in a fragmented way. By following the principle of clause 6, issues around role demarcation (who does what in the practice) and dealing with confidentiality can be dealt with. Practice nurses can also use clause 6 to stress the importance of proper team meetings in which they can make a valued contribution.

Clause 14 is slightly different, in that it describes how nurses must:

*'...assist professional colleagues, in the context of your own knowledge, experience and sphere of responsibility, to develop their professional competence, and assist others in the care team, including informal carers, to contribute safely and to a degree appropriate to their roles;'*

There are two strands to this requirement. First, it is your responsibility to pass on your expertise to other colleagues, and also to help them source the additional skills and information they may need to develop their practice. In this respect the clause is particularly relevant to those nurses who have managerial responsibility for others, although the principle should be the same among colleagues working at the same level.

The second strand is the involvement of informal carers in the team. There is some debate as to the accountability of nurses who have taught relatives how to undertake a particular aspect of care which hitherto was performed by a nurse. The situation is that nurses giving instruction should do so with regard to this clause, i.e. they should teach the carers properly and ensure that they are able to do the job safely. The individual nurse must decide, for each situation, which activities can be taught to, and performed by, the carer.

## Integrity

Several clauses within the *Code of Professional Conduct* reflect an expectation of integrity on the part of registered nurses, so far as their interaction with patients is concerned, but clauses 15 and 16 deal with this issue by referring to the need for nurses to be beyond reproach so far as professional standards are concerned.

Clause 15 indicates that you must:

*'...refuse any gift, favour or hospitality from patients or clients currently in your care which might be interpreted as seeking to exert influence to obtain preferential consideration;'*

The UKCC is not saying that nurses should not accept tokens of gratitude, but rather that the providers of gifts should not be treated any differently.

Perhaps more important than the risk of bribery is the delicate situation in which a nurse can be placed if, having been given a gift, there is no way that the nurse could alter the situation to the benefit of the patient, even if she/he wanted to. The patient or relative could come to see the nurse as ungrateful, or even uncaring. It is best to consider each situation on its own merits; nobody wants to upset a patient who offers small gifts, but perhaps offers of a more generous nature could be diverted to the purchase of an item of practice equipment, or a donation to a health-related charity.

The final clause of the *Code*, clause 16, outlines the consideration that nurses must give to the use of their registration status:

*'ensure that your registration status is not used in the promotion of commercial products or services, declare any financial or other interests in relevant organisations providing such goods or services and ensure that your professional judgement is not influenced by any commercial considerations.'*

You might think that it is very unlikely that you would use your status in this way, but consider the items you may use in your practice. Do you write advice to give to patients on a pad provided by a drug company with its logo on the bottom? Do you give out free samples which might have been given to you for professional interest? When you recommend that a patient buys a certain product from the chemist, is that because it is the best option or because the representative for the company who makes it had visited you that morning? These examples might seem petty, but you must bear in mind this clause when engaging in such activity.

Not quite so vague are those situations where nurses may have a vested interest in organisations providing care to patients. For example, the practice nurse whose partner runs a nursing home would have to take care in recommending that home to a patient or carers. Sometimes a nurse may unwittingly endorse a service, and be accused of favouritism. On such an occasion a minicab company complained to an FHSA that a practice nurse always recommended a rival company. Word got around that the company was particularly good at dealing with patients — because the nurse recommended it — and the business of competitors plummeted. The practice nurse concerned had no financial interests in the recommended cab company, but found herself having to apologise to its rivals. Never underestimate the authority which can be vested in your status as a registered nurse.

## Summary of the *Code*

The UKCC *Code of Professional Conduct* is a tiny three-page document, only a few hundred words long, but it is **your** contract with the profession. The *Code* is a powerful document and contains the standards by which your practice will be judged; it outlines the extent of your accountability.

Daunting as it may seem, the *Code* was not devised as means of restricting nursing practice, or as a 'big stick' with which to beat those who deviate from the professional ideal. The *Code* is a tool to be used by all nurses, and it can both liberate practice and provide you with the ammunition you need to ensure that the care you deliver, and your patients receive, is always of the highest possible standard. If you read, understand and apply it, you have nothing to fear from being a truly accountable practitioner.

## The Scope of Professional Practice

### Background

Second only in importance to the *Code of Professional Conduct*, *The Scope of Professional Practice* (UKCC, 1992b) is probably the most significant publication of recent years relating to the practice of nursing. The *Scope* recognises the emergence of professionalism within nursing, and sets out to liberate practice.

From the late 1970s it was becoming obvious that nurses were able to extend their work into new areas. Davis (1992) explains that the extended role was generally defined as one that encompasses activities not included in basic nurse training, and is usually carried out by a doctor. Nurses began to undertake such tasks as routine cervical screening in general practice, the performance of ECGs, insertion of intravenous cannulae, blood sampling, etc. However this role extension was carried out with strict reference to, and authorisation by, the medical profession. This is reflected in the original extended role guidance issued by the Chief Nursing and Chief Medical Officers of the time (DHSS, 1977), which clearly stated that it was the responsibility of doctors to ensure that nurses were competent to accept delegated duties. This determination of competence was backed up by an anachronistic system in which certificates of competence were issued once nurses had been judged to be competent to undertake that for which they were being assessed.

As nursing developed further through the 1980s, there was a growing move away from the idea of extended roles, and the notion of these being sanctioned by doctors (Clay 1987). Nursing organisations such as the RCN lobbied the Department of Health and the new UKCC, to the effect that the extended role guidance should be reviewed and withdrawn, making the responsibility for defining new roles the remit of the nursing profession. This movement culminated in the publication of *The Scope of Professional Practice* in June 1992.

### Key points

The content of the *Scope* can be summarised in four key points. It:
- *Abolishes the extended role*
- *Emphasises personal accountability*
- *Enables role expansion linked to competence*

- *Underlines the need for education.*

## Abolition of the extended role

As discussed above, the profession had come to see the extended role concept as too limited and a constraint to practice, encumbered by the system of competence determination. The introduction to the *Scope* acknowledges that:

> 'The practice of nursing, midwifery and health visiting requires the application
> of knowledge and the simultaneous exercise of judgement and skill. Practice takes
> place in a context of continuing change and development...Practice must,
> therefore, be sensitive, relevant and responsive to the needs of individual patients
> and clients and have the capacity to adjust, where and when appropriate, to
> changing circumstances.'

UKCC, 1992b, section 1:01)

In issuing the *Scope* guidance, the UKCC was seeking to inform the development of a nursing profession which could live up to this challenge. It recognised that this could not be achieved if widening and enhancing nursing practice was only possible through 'official' extension of that role by certification. The Council was adamant that:

> '...the terms "extended" or "extending" roles which have been associated with this
> system are no longer suitable since they limit, rather than extend, the parameters
> of practice. As a result, many practitioners have been prevented from fulfilling
> their potential for the benefit of patients...'

(UKCC, 1992b, section 13:08)

## Emphasis on personal accountability

If we remove the restricting and outdated principles of extended role certification, some means of determining how nurses should expand their role is needed to replace them. The UKCC was, and still is, of the opinion that all registered nurses should be sufficiently accountable for their actions, that they would only add activities to their skill base if they believed they were competent to carry them out to a satisfactory standard:

> 'In order to bring into proper focus the professional responsibility and consequent
> accountability of individual practitioners, it is the Council's principles for
> practice rather than certificates for tasks which should form the basis for
> adjustments to the scope of practice.'

(UKCC, 1992b, section 14:09)

In making this statement, the UKCC clearly refers back to the *Code of Professional Conduct*, as does most of the *Scope* document, emphasising the link between autonomy, responsibility and accountability as discussed earlier. Under the terms of the *Scope* guidance, the UKCC provides the authority through which nurses are free to expand their roles as they see fit, with the proviso that they are willing to accept full responsibility and be accountable for anything they do in the context of such expansion.

## Expansion linked to competence

In the *Scope* document, the UKCC is very specific in making the link between role expansion linked to competence as defined in the *Code of Professional Conduct*. The *Scope* specifically cites clauses 1–4 of the *Code*, which we know, from our previous discussion, requires nurses to ensure that their practice is up to date, that they only undertake activities for which they know they are competent, and that they always act in a manner which is in the best interest of patients. We can consider the *Scope* to be a document which facilitates role expansion, but as its states:

> *'The Code provides a firm bedrock upon which decisions about adjustments to the scope of professional practice can be made.'*

(UKCC, 1992b: Section 7: 05).

## Education for expansion

In setting out its guidance for role expansion through the *Scope*, the UKCC underlines the importance of proper education before nurses take on new roles. This is linked to the competency proviso, in that individual nurses are charged with ensuring that they have the knowledge to provide care to a satisfactory standard. The *Scope* details how a nurse must:

> *'...honestly acknowledge any limits of personal knowledge and skill and take steps to remedy any relevant deficits in order effectively and appropriately to meet the needs of patients and clients.'*

(UKCC, 1992b, section 9.3:06)

This is a clear reference to clause 4 of the *Code of Professional Conduct*, but here the emphasis is on the personal responsibility of nurses to ensure that they have received the education needed to expand their role in a particular way.

Similarly, the UKCC is clear that it does not expect nurses to be able to expand their role based upon their basic training, and that additional learning will be required:

> *'This foundation education alone, however, cannot effectively meet the changing and complex demands of the range of modern health care. Post-registration education equips practitioners with additional and more specialist skills necessary to meet the special needs of patients and clients.'*

(UKCC, 1992b, section 3:03)

Although this is a matter of individual responsibility, it is reasonable for a practice nurse to expect that the employer — the GP partners — would assist in this. However, there is always the potential for a differing interpretation as to what steps need to be taken to remedy the deficiency in a nurse's knowledge base. See case study 4 (page 83) for a discussion of this issue.

## The nature of expanded practice

We could debate at great length the nature of nursing practice, and whether or not role expansion actually turns nurses into mini-doctors, or equips them with a whole range of new skills with which they can deliver a superlative level of service to patients.

As nursing has moved forward, it has encompassed an increasing number of activities within its role, and the test must be whether those activities which are brought in add to the potential of the nurse to deliver a better package of nursing care. A good example would be the taking of cervical smears. Only 10–15 years ago, GPs had the responsibility of taking smears, yet the practice nurse would consult with the patient concerning her general health status, and explain the procedure, only for that patient to be passed on to the doctor. This fragmented pattern of care was solved by giving nurses the skills needed to take over this activity. A medical skill was legitimately incorporated into nursing practice, as this provided an enhanced standard of care which was well within the remit of nursing.

Within the *Scope*, the UKCC offers guidance on this, stating that nurses must:

> '...ensure that any enlargement or adjustment of the scope of professional practice must be achieved without compromising or fragmenting existing aspects of professional practice and care and that the requirements of the Council's Code of Professional Conduct are satisfied throughout the whole area of practice.'

(UKCC, 1992b, section 9.4:07)

Case study 12 (page 125) explains how role expansion should proceed according to this guidance by discussing a couple of practice nurses who, unfortunately, did not get it quite right.

## Summary

On a quick first read the two key UKCC texts, the *Code of Professional Conduct*, and *The Scope of Professional Practice*, seem to be a set of rules imposed upon the profession, through which we will be judged. However, a thorough examination of these documents reveals that while they do indeed set out the parameters for our practice, they provide the tools we need in exercising our accountability and ensuring high quality nursing care. The *Scope* in particular is one of, if not **the**, most liberating document in recent nursing history, transferring the responsibility for expanding the nature of nursing practice back to the profession, and to practitioners themselves.

Armed with an understanding of these documents and how they relate to day-to-day work, practice nurses are equipped to develop their practice to the highest possible level.

### *Action Points*

* ✳ *Check that you have a copy of the* **Code** *and* **Scope**, *and read them through.*
* ✳ *Set some time aside at your practice nurse group meeting to consider the implications of the* **Code** *and* **Scope**.
* ✳ *Suggest that the* **Code** *and* **Scope** *are the subject of a practice meeting.*
* ✳ *Test your practice against the* **Code** *and guidance within the* **Scope**.

## Key Texts

Pyne RH (1992) *Professional Conduct and Discipline in Nursing, Midwifery and Health Visiting.* Blackwell Scientific Publications London

UKCC (1992) *Code of Professional Conduct.* UKCC, London

UKCC (1992) *The Scope of Professional Practice.* UKCC, London

UKCC (1996) *Ethical Guidelines for Professional Practice.* UKCC, London

## References

Clay T (1987) *Nurses, Power and Politics.* Heinemann, London

Daily Mail (1991) Brake on Nurse (news item). Daily Mail 3 August: 15

Davis J (1992) Expanding Horizons. *Nursing Times* **88**(47): 37–9

DHSS (1977) *The Extended Role of the Nurse,* HC (77) 22. HMSO, London

Pyne R (1992a) The Code of Conduct (UKCC Code of Conduct's guidance on accountability). *Practice Nursing* July/August: 12

Pyne R (1992b) Breaking the Code. *Nursing* **5**(3): 8–10

Pyne R (1994) Professional conduct and accountability. *Modern Midwife* **4**(9): 15–7

UKCC (1992a) *Code of Professional Conduct.* UKCC, London

UKCC (1992b) *The Scope of Professional Practice.* UKCC, London

UKCC (1996) *Ethical Guidelines for Professional Practice.* UKCC, London

## Further reading

Ashcroft J (1992) Rising to the challenge. (The implications for the nursing role of the UKCC document *The Scope of Professional Practice*). *Nursing Times* **88**(37): 30

Carlisle D (1992) Scope for extensions. (Replacing the extended role guidance with *The Scope of Professional Practice*). *Nursing Times* **88**(37): 26–8

Derrick S (1989) What are the legal implications of extended nursing roles? *Professional Nurse* **4**(7): 350–2

Dimond B (1991) All part of the job. (Legal problems of incorporating the UKCC code of conduct within employment contracts). *Nursing Times* **87**(33): 44–6

Lunn J (1994) The scope of professional practice for a legal perspective. *Br J Nursing* **3**(15): 770–2

Moores Y (1992) Setting new boundaries (Comments on the *The Scope of Professional Practice*). *Nursing Times* **88**(37): 28–9

Rea K (1992) The UKCC code deciphered, (Legal and professional implications of the revised code of conduct). *Nursing Standard* **6**(50): 51–4

Tingle J (1990) Responsible and liable? (Legal issues surrounding the extended role). *Nursing Times* **86**(25): 42–3

# Chapter 4
# When Things Go Wrong — Regulating the Profession

## Key Issues and Concepts:

- An overview of the regulatory mechanism of the nursing profession
- The differences between various forms of alleged misconduct
- The UKCC Professional Conduct Committee
- Professional regulation in the context of ill-health

*'The United Kingdom Central Council for Nursing, Midwifery and Health Visiting is the statutory body responsible for regulating nursing, midwifery and health visiting throughout the United Kingdom. The Council is charged by Parliament with the duty to establish and improve standards of training and professional conduct for nurses, midwives and health visitors. The means of regulation include determining the standards for entry to the professions, standards for education, and for conduct. The right to practise is conferred by the Council by registration and this right may be removed only by the Council'.*

(UKCC, 1990)

This extract is taken from the introduction to the UKCC's (1990) publication '...*with a view to removal from the register*...', the title of which is taken from the Statutory Rules of the Council governing its professional conduct duties (see page 44). This publication explains the process through which the UKCC exercises the ultimate test of accountability, i.e. a hearing before the Professional Conduct Committee (PCC). I sincerely hope that no reader will find themselves heading in the direction of the PCC (this book is intended to help with that), let alone having their registration revoked, but it is useful to consider the workings of this Committee, and to see how nurses come to its attention.

Although the way in which the UKCC deals with alleged misconduct might just be of interest, and the study of it serve to sharpen up your practice, you may also need to consider whether you need to make an allegation yourself. Remember that the *Code of Professional Conduct* requires you to speak out if you suspect misconduct on the part of a colleague who is on the register. We are not talking about simple problems, which should be talked through and dealt with in the practice, but about instances where you think someone is acting in a way that could be construed as misconduct. Reporting such instances should not be seen as mere 'whistleblowing', but as a professional duty. This overview will also help you to exercise that duty if — as unappealing as it may be — you are obliged to do so.

## The UKCC committee structure

The PCC machinery of the UKCC is governed by section 12 of the Nurses, Midwives and Health Visitors Act 1979, which requires the Council to make statutory rules governing the circumstances in which nurses can be removed from the register. These rules are known as the Professional Conduct Rules, and are described in Statutory Instrument 1987, No.2156 for England, Scotland and Wales, and Statutory Instrument 1987, No 473 for Northern Ireland. These rules require the Council to organise committees made up of its members in order to consider allegations of misconduct. This committee is the Professional Conduct Committee. The Council is also required to set up two other committees, again drawn from its members: one of these is the Panel of Screeners and the other is the Health Committee. Together these two committees consider whether allegations that an individual may not be fit to practise are due to reasons of ill-health.

## How are complaints alleging misconduct made?

You will remember that the prime function of the UKCC is to protect the public interest. It follows then that any member of the public is free to make allegations of misconduct to the Council. Additionally, any colleague, whether nursing, medical, or from another professional group, might decide that your action is worthy of being judged in terms of misconduct. In short, anyone can make an allegation to the UKCC calling into question your continued status as a registered nurse (see*Figure 4-2* for a schematic representation of the process).

Many complaints alleging misconduct arise after a nurse has been through a criminal court where guilt has been proven. The UKCC has agreed systems through which any nurse who has been through the court in this way will be directly reported to the Council by that court or the police. Even though this is the case, anyone who knows that a nurse has been to court, and has been found guilty of an offence which could call into question his/her future registration, is free to report this to the Council.

In whatever circumstances the incident occurred which gave rise to the complaint, whether this was passage through a court, the suspicion of a colleague, or an allegation from a patient resulting from an episode of care, the complaint should be made in writing to the investigating office for the National Board for Nursing, Midwifery and Health Visiting, appropriate for the country in which the nurse concerned is living or working. The letter should set out the details of the complaint, and provide as much information as is available to help identify the nurse on the register.

It is worth remembering here that the UKCC committee dealing with alleged misconduct is not intended to be a means of punishing practitioners (although if you have your name removed from the register you might think so), or of providing employers with grounds to dismiss a nurse. Also, the UKCC route is not another means of 'having a go' at a nurse if appeals against internal disciplinary measures have been upheld. Note also that the nurse who makes an allegation of misconduct to the Council to 'get her own back' is acting in a way which is certainly in breach of the *Code of Professional Conduct* if nothing

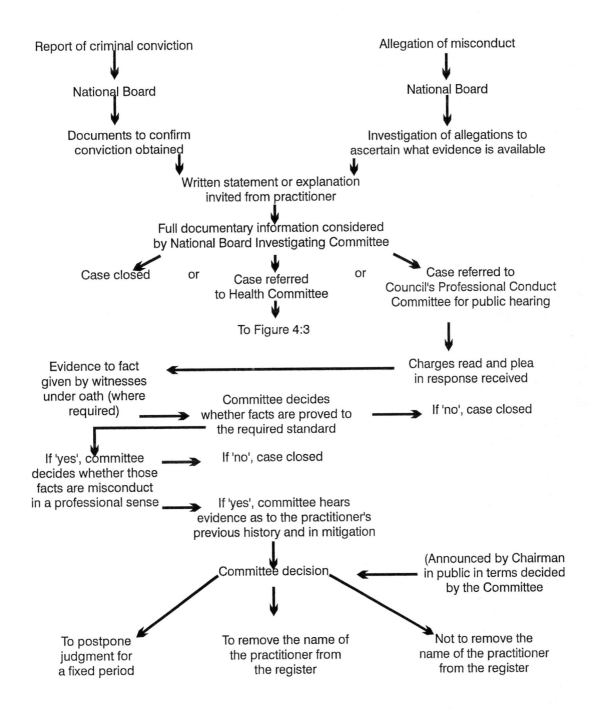

**Figure 4-2  A simplified illustration of the process by which an allegation of misconduct is considered (After UKCC, 1990)**

happened to warrant that complaint. The UKCC will take a very dim view and serious action against nurses who use it to settle scores with colleagues.

In pursuance of the investigation, the nurse against whom an allegation has been made will be informed of this and asked for a written statement, explanation or comment. Any nurse finding his/herself in this situation would be wise to contact his/her representative organisation for advice before making a response. Once the investigating officer at the National Board has considered the allegation, the case may then be referred to the Council for the attention of the PCC. Not all cases will be referred as some may not have sufficient grounds, some may be malicious, and the facts backing up some complaints may be exceedingly spurious. Additionally, if it is determined that the allegations are indicative of illness, the case may be referred to the UKCC Health Committee (see case study 7, page 101).

## Case referred to the PCC

If a case is passed on, evidence in support of the allegation of misconduct must be given by witnesses testifying under oath in a public hearing. These public hearings of the PCC are held around the UK, and are open to anyone. It is a useful exercise to attend one in order to see how your profession deals with colleagues who are alleged to be in breach of the *Code of Professional Conduct*. Arrangements to attend can be made through the UKCC.

The standards of evidence and proof required by the PCC are the same as those which apply in the criminal courts. Something overheard in a corridor, or a supposition based on something told to you by a colleague, will not be good enough. Rather than such 'hearsay' evidence, the PCC will need hard fact, and anyone alleging misconduct can only do so on the basis of what they know to be true. Similarly, the PCC cannot judge whether any allegation is proven on the basis of mere probability. The committee members have to be sure beyond any reasonable doubt before taking action as serious as removing someone's name from the register.

In making its decision, the PCC considers several key points:

- The purpose of the hearing is to concentrate on the matters which feature in the charges formally notified to the nurse concerned, and not to elicit evidence of other unsatisfactory behaviour.
- It is essential that the incident, if proven to the required standard, is considered in the context of its occurrence rather than in isolation.
- Information about the previous history of the nurse involved is extremely important. It sometimes emerges that the incident in question occurred when the pressure of work was severe, that the nurse concerned was immediately honest and open about it, and that a previous record extending over many years was exemplary.

Also, if during the PCC hearing, evidence becomes available indicating that the practitioner concerned could have been ill at the time the alleged breach of the *Code of Professional Conduct* occurred, the committee can decide to refer the case to the Health Committee. This route is discussed later.

## What offences could lead to a nurse being 'struck off'?

Bearing in mind that the purpose of the Conduct Committees of the UKCC is not to punish nurses, but rather to protect publish interest, the types of offence that are likely to lead to removal of one's name from the register are those which, in the opinion of the PCC, reflect an image of a nurse who is either dangerous in practice, or unlikely to change her/his behaviour following a warning or caution. Frequently occurring reasons for removal from the register are:

- Reckless and wilfully unskilful practice
- Concealing untoward incidents
- Failure to keep essential records
- Falsifying records
- Failure to protect or promote the interests of patients
- Failure to act knowing that a colleague or subordinate is improperly treating or abusing patients
- Physical or verbal abuse of patients
- Abuse of patients by improperly withholding prescribed drugs, or administering non-prescribed drugs or an excess of prescribed drugs
- Theft from patients or employers
- Drug-related offences
- Sexual abuse of patients
- Breach of confidentiality

(UKCC, 1990)

Although this is a pretty long list, it is obvious that the offences described are of a serious nature. You can also see that they are closely related to the 16 clauses of the *Code*, and common sense indicates that if a nurse makes a serious breach of one of those clauses, without mitigating circumstances, then that breach has a greater chance of leading to removal from the register.

Although we would not want to consider it as a list of 'what you can get away with', the UKCC has also indicated some offences which, although they could come to the attention of a PCC, would be unlikely to result in a nurse being struck off. These are as follows:

- Offences related to motor vehicles
- Issues that relate specifically to employment, such as leaving work early without permission, falsifying overtime claims and mistakes admitted by the practitioner due to pressure of work
- Cases where the practitioner's failure was effectively failure to achieve the impossible in the circumstances that applied
- Cases in which a nurse had thought through his/her actions using professional judgment, and acted in a way that could be justified as being reasonable at the time

- Situations where the complaint has been brought against the practitioner, measuring practice against outdated practices and norms.

(UKCC, 1990)

Additionally, even when cases which have been before the PCC have had the alleged misconduct proven, there may be situations in which the decision is taken not to remove the nurse's name from the register. These include:

- The incident was isolated and uncharacteristic, and the practitioner appears to have learnt from the experience
- At the time of the misconduct, there were overwhelming personal problems causing the practitioner to behave inappropriately, and these have now been resolved
- The practitioner has been kept in employment and has had good reports since the incident of misconduct
- Having been responsible for an error, the practitioner made no attempt to hide it, and immediately reported it in the interests of the patient
- With hindsight, it was clear that the incident was an error of professional misjudgment rather than a culpable act
- The practitioner was one of a number involved, but the only person to be complained about
- Removal from the register would be too harsh a response to the established facts
- Senior managers, at the time of the incident, were aware that the environment of care was such that the pressures on staff were great, but took no action to remedy the situation.

(UKCC, 1990)

## Complaints alleging unfitness to practise due to illness

We briefly discussed earlier the possibility that the investigating officer of the National Board considering a complaint which could lead to an offence of misconduct was also able to make a preliminary decision as to whether the alleged offence was the result of a nurse being ill at the time it happened. Where such concerns emerge during the investigation of a complaint, or at PCC stage, the case becomes a matter for formal record and immediate transfer for consideration on health grounds (see *Figure 3* for a schematic representation of the process). In this context, 'ill health' relates to both physical and mental health problems.

In addition to this route of referral due to ill health, anyone can express concern and begin the process through which a practitioner's possible unfitness to practise due to illness will be assessed and a decision made about their registration status. Such an expression of concern should be made direct to the UKCC, rather than a National Board.

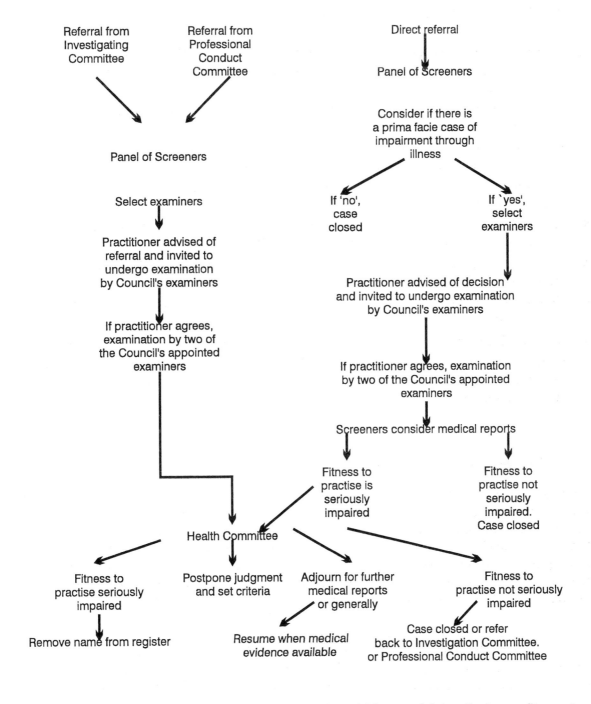

**Figure 4-3** A simplified illustration of the process by which complaints alleging unfitness to practise are considered (after UKCC, 1990)

## The direct referral case

A direct referral to the UKCC should be made by letter to the Assistant Registrar for Professional Conduct (this title may change in the future) giving brief details of the known illness or symptomatic behaviour causing concern, together with sufficient information to enable the Council to identify the practitioner. Using this letter, the Council's solicitor will draft a statutory declaration for the person making the referral to sign. This is required by law, and without it an investigation of the practitioner's alleged unfitness to practise cannot proceed.

Once the statutory declaration has been signed and returned to the Council, the case is formally opened and considered by a group of Council members (the Panel of Screeners) who look at the written evidence and decide whether the case should be pursued or closed. If the decision is to pursue, the Screeners decide on the category of specialist medical examiners they wish the practitioner to be referred to.

## A case referred from an investigating committee or PCC

The decision that the practitioner's fitness to practise is questionable will already have been decided by the referring committee. In this case the role of the Screeners will be limited to the selection of the category of medical examiners.

## The health committee hearing

Before the hearing takes place, the practitioner concerned will have seen the appropriate medical examiners, usually in an area close to where they live, but not in the same area as the practitioner lives or works. The reports from the examinations are made available to the practitioner and to the committee members.

Because of the sensitivity of the material being considered, the public hearing rules of the PCC do not apply, and the Health Committee meets in private. The Committee for each case comprises five Council members assisted by a Council officer and a legal assessor. One of the medical examiners contributing to the reports before the Committee also has to be present. The practitioner is also encouraged to attend, and can be represented by a person or organisation of his/her choice, and may also bring a friend and medical advisers.

The UKCC reports that in the majority of cases the practitioner accepts the general findings of the medical reports and allows them to form the basis of discussion within the Health Committee hearing (UKCC, 1990). There may be rare occasions in direct referral cases, where the practitioner has refused to see the medical examiners appointed by the Council, and has exercised the right to ask that the persons making the allegations, together with witnesses to the behaviour which resulted in the allegations, attend the hearing. In such a case, one or more of the medical examiners drawn from the Council's panel will attend in the capacity of medical assessor and advise the Committee.

Since the Health Committee commenced its work in 1984, the conditions which have most frequently led to the removal of practitioners' names from the register have been alcohol dependence, dependence on drugs, and various mental health problems (UKCC, 1990).

## Summary

The UKCC takes its statutory responsibilities seriously in the maintenance of professional standards within our profession, for the public good. However, even though this is the prime responsibility, the PCC and Health Committee do have the interest of nurses at heart. The fact that a case has been reported to the National Board, and then on to the PCC, does not automatically mean that the nurse is heading for professional ruin. Rather, the UKCC has made sure that all cases will be examined on their own merits and where appropriate, and, while still keeping the interest of the public at the centre, will deal with the nurse in a way that encourages a change in practice rather than bringing an end to that practice.

Accountability to one's own professional group, through an ethical code such as our *Code of Professional Conduct*, is indeed the marker of a true profession. Through the UKCC we have that accountability combined with the wider accountability to the public. These are real strengths at the core of nursing.

### *Action Points*

* *Consider the differences in alleged professional misconduct due to deliberate act, oversight, obvious incompetence and ill health.*
* *Using the case study examples in Part II, how do you think a Professional Conduct Committee would have responded to them?*
* *Arrange to attend a public hearing of the Professional Conduct Committee.*

# References

UKCC (1990) '...*with a view to removal from the register...*' *An Explanation of the System for Considering Complaints against Registered Nurses, Midwives and Health Visitors which Call Into Question their Appropriateness to Practise.* UKCC, London

# Further reading

Morrison I (1987) Reviewing the evidence, (Author's experiences of serving as a member of the UKCC Professional Conduct Committee). *Nursing Times and Nursing Mirror* **83**(8): 31–3

Vousden M (1987) Conduct unbecoming, (Review of professional conduct committee's statistics). *Nursing Times and Nursing Mirror* **83**(8): 33–4

UKCC Register (1989) Explaining the UKCC's work, (UKCC Professional Conduct Committee).*UKCC Register No 5*: 4

# Chapter 5
# Accountability in a Legal Context

## Key Issues and Concepts

- The relationship between professional accountability and the law
- Accountability through the civil and crown courts
- Negligence and the duty of care

*'However accountability is defined and whatever the value of ethical codes it is important to remember that the courts are the final venue for the resolution of disputes in medicine and nursing. This fact should make the acquiring of some legal knowledge, as it relates to nursing, a professional priority for every nurse'.*

(Tingle, 1990)

In the vast majority of disputes between patient and nurse, local arrangements such as practice complaints procedures, which allow patients to make their case and the nurse to apologise for whatever was done to upset them, will be sufficient. Similarly, disagreement between employer and employee will generally be resolved by discussion and compromise, or through formal disciplinary and grievance systems. However, as Tingle (1990) indicates, all such disputes could move to the final arbiter — the court of law.

Dimond (1989) includes two aspects of the legal system alongside the employer and the profession as the core components of professional accountability (Figure 4). She indicates that a nurse may be held to account through some legal process, either through a civil court, where a patient asks that a judgment about standards of practice and professional behaviour be made on his/her behalf, or through a criminal court, where the wider interests of society are addressed, and it is determined whether the action of a nurse was or was not a crime against that society.

Dimond attests that there is no moral difference between the two court processes, only that a breach of criminal law can be followed by prosecution in the criminal courts, whereas liability in civil law is actionable in the civil courts and may or may not constitute a crime. Some actions may be both criminal and civil wrongdoings, and may be followed by both civil and criminal proceedings.

## Supernurse?

Before we consider the process of accountability through the civil and criminal systems of our legal system, we should first consider the standard by which professional practice will

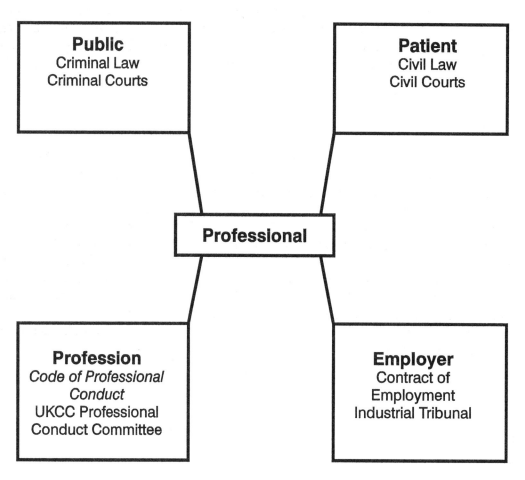

**Figure 5-4** Arenas of accountability (after Dimond, 1990)

be judged. This is particularly important in view of the fact that scores of practice nurses contact the RCN simply to obtain reassurance that their practice is 'good enough'.

In law, the reference point is the Bolam test. You may already be aware that a substantial part of our law is based upon previous cases and how a judge has ruled upon them, i.e. case law. In the Bolam test, the case between Bolam (a doctor) and his employing authority, the Management Committee of Friern Barnet Hospital, determines the standard of care which can be expected of a professional person. The test can be summarised as follows:

> *'When you get a situation which involves the use of some special skill or competence, then the test as to whether there has been negligence or not is ...the standard of the ordinary skilled man exercising and professing to have that special skill. If a surgeon failed to measure up to that in any respect ('clinical judgement' or otherwise) he had been negligent and should be so adjudged'.*

> (Whitehouse v. Jordan [1981])

This argument has equal weight with other professional groups, and basically means that the courts will judge professional competence as being the level of skill practised by other average members of that profession. A practice nurse accused of negligence would therefore, have his/her standard of care measured against a group of average practice nurses, not some supernurse exhibiting the highest standard of practice in the land.

## Civil cases

Civil law concerns the responsibilities we have to one another, and the rights we have as individuals within society. For example, if a patient is dissatisfied with the level of care received, and believes that the standard was such that the nurse concerned was negligent, then that patient could take legal action in the civil courts. The outcome of such an action would be a financial one, i.e. if the court believed that the patient had been wronged, it would award financial compensation of an amount it considered to be worthy of any suffering caused. In coming to such a decision the court would have to form the opinion that the nurse concerned was in breach of a statutory duty to provide care to an acceptable standard (see Chapter 2 for discussion of the UKCC's statutory role in issuing the *Code of Professional Conduct*), and that harm had come to the patient as a result.

Negligence is but one example of a civil wrong — a tort — which could be dealt with in the civil courts. Others would include:

- Trespass — to property, to land, and to the person
- False imprisonment
- Wrongful interference
- Breach of statutory duty
- Nuisance
- Defamation
- Malicious prosecution
- Deliberate interference with interests in trade or business.

Obviously not all of these are relevant to nursing practice, and negligence is by far the most common in respect of that practice. When considering the case studies in Part II, give some thought as to what particular civil wrongs the nurses involved in those cases could have been accused of.

Whatever the nature of the wrong, if found in favour of the person who has been wronged, i.e. the plaintiff, an award is made against whom the action was taken. This could be the nurse or the employer who may have been found to be vicariously liable.

Vicarious liability is an important point to consider, in that the law will see that whoever was providing care to the patient who was harmed is negligent, e.g. the practice nurse. However, legal responsibility for negligence can be placed on the employer, i.e. the GP, who in law has a responsibility to ensure that a satisfactory standard of care is being provided by employees. This point often leads to confusion concerning the concept of 'being covered'.

Practice nurses commonly consult the RCN over this issue, and many report that GPs have indicated that it is all right for them[the nurses] to undertake a particular activity as they [the GPs] will 'cover' them. Clearly, as the GP can be held vicariously liable, he/she does 'cover' the nurse to a certain extent. But in civil law, the liability of the employer does not wipe out the liability of the employee. Although civil law holds that an employer may well be sued instead of the employee, each may be found to be negligent, and each could be sued. It is therefore appropriate that both employing GP and employed practice nurse have some form of indemnity insurance to offset any successful claims or legal expenses awarded against them.

We should also note here that even if civil law holds that an employing GP can be answerable for a charge of negligence against an employed practice nurse, this is where professional accountability and legal accountability diverge. Even if the GP wanted to take the full blame for the practice nurse's actions, it will be the nurse who is answerable to the UKCC Professional Conduct Committee. Also, civil law, with respect to negligence, requires that a harm has been done, but this is not the case with professional accountability, and misconduct may well be alleged in the absence of such a harm. Above all, remember that professional accountability is a personal thing and nobody other than you can be answerable for your actions.

## Criminal cases

We are probably more familiar with the way in which criminal cases are progressed, from the media and police soaps on television. A review of the course of criminal proceedings is useful, as any nurse may well find him/herself involved as a witness, if not he accused.

The first point to acknowledge is that the reference points are different from those of the civil court, in that the accused is assumed innocent until proved otherwise, and proof has to be determined beyond reasonable doubt. Upon arrest under suspicion of a crime, the rules contained within PACE (the Police and Criminal Evidence Act 1984) apply. PACE provides guidelines concerning the detention, treatment and questioning of people by the police and must be made available in police stations. PACE applies equally to those who have been arrested, or simply agreed to voluntarily go to a police station to help with enquiries (see Zander, 1995 for a comprehensive review of PACE).

A person accused of a crime could be arrested at the scene, somewhere else upon their later apprehension, or once taken to the police station. Wherever the arrest takes place, the accused must be given the caution:

> *'You do not have to say anything. But it may harm your defence if you do not mention when questioned something which you later rely on in court. Anything you say may be given in evidence'.*

Accused persons are also advised of their right to have a solicitor. If they have been arrested in the context of their nursing work, rather than for a non-nursing offence, they may wish to notify their representative organisation, who can in turn appoint an appropriate solicitor, rather than rely on the services of the duty solicitor whom the police can make available. If only the duty solicitor is available, it is wise to take up this option. Once cautioned, the next step is for the police officer(s) concerned to attempt to establish the facts through a taped interview. Once the police are of the opinion that they have obtained sufficient evidence to prosecute a detained suspect, that individual has to be brought before the custody officer who then decides whether or not he/she should be charged with a crime.

Once seen by the custody officer, the accused must be given a further caution together with a written notice detailing the offence with which he/she has been charged, the name of the arresting officer and the police station at which he/she is based. Once charged, no further questions may be put to the accused relating to the case. If further questions need to be asked, e.g. to minimise harm or loss to other persons, or to clear up a misunderstanding surrounding a previous answer in the light of fresh information, then a further caution must be given before doing so. Note that it is now the responsibility of the Crown Prosecution Service (CPS) to decide whether or not criminal proceedings are instituted against an accused individual.

## The criminal courts

Dimond indicates that almost all criminal cases begin in the magistrates' court and that 90% of all cases are concluded there (Dimond, 1990). Some offences can only be tried by judge and jury. These are known as indictable offences and include murder, causing death by reckless driving, robbery and wounding by intent. Even if the case is considered appropriate to the magistrates court, the accused is still given the opportunity of trial by judge and jury in the crown courts. If the accused opts for the crown court, the magistrates act as examining justices and decide whether there is sufficient evidence for the case to proceed.

If the case is to be tried by magistrates and the plea is a guilty one, the case will probably be heard there and then; if a not guilty plea is to be entered, it is likely that the case will be adjourned and a date set for a full hearing. Once the case is heard, the magistrates will determine whether the accused is guilty or not, and pass an appropriate sentence. Magistrates are only given limited sentencing powers, and if they believe that they are unable to give a sentence that reflects the severity of the crime, they may well refer the case to the crown court for sentencing.

Should the accused be committed to the crown court, then the case will be heard by judge and jury, with representation by counsel, i.e. a barrister. the charges are put to the accused, who again can plead guilty or not guilty. If a not guilty plea is entered then the trial will open with a short address by the prosecution counsel, describing the key elements the prosecution will have to prove. The prosecution then calls witnesses to prove its case. These witnesses are examined 'in chief' which means that they cannot be asked leading questions. Once questioned by the prosecution, the defence can cross-examine the witnesses, this time asking leading questions designed to discredit the evidence or show it to be irrelevant. After defence cross-examination, the prosecution can re-examine the witness once more to pick up on points raised in the cross-examination. After this last examination of prosecution witnesses has finished, the judge has the right to close the case if it is felt that there is insufficient evidence to substantiate the prosecution's case.

If the judge allows the case to continue, the defence can call its witnesses, The accused does not have to appear as a witness, but if they do, they must answer all questions, even those which might incriminate them. After all evidence is complete, the defence and prosecution conclude their cases in one last address to the court. The judge then sums up the case for the jury and, bearing in mind that this is composed of members of the general public, explains the elements of the crime which the prosecution should have shown to have been committed by the defendant. The jury then selects a foreman and retires to consider its verdict based on the evidence heard.

Initially the jury is asked to give a unanimous verdict, but if it looks likely that this will be impossible, the judge will consider the majority opinion. If the jury decides that the defendant is innocent, then he/she is free to leave the court. If the defendant is found guilty, then details of past convictions and social circumstances are made available to court, and the judge will pass sentence, usually within accepted guidelines. The defendant still has the right to appeal against the way in which the trial was conducted, or against the severity of the sentence.

A detailed account of the arrest and interview process, and the court systems as related to nursing practice, can be found in *Legal Aspects of Nursing* (Dimond, 1990).

## Summary

This might all sound a little heavy for a book which purports to be a practical guide to issues of accountability in practice nursing, but even though the odds are very much against it, you never know when you might become embroiled in this process — if only as a witness. Furthermore, even if a nurse has been through a trial by jury in the crown court, the UKCC still has to put its Professional Conduct Committee mechanism into operation. Although it might not be the most pressing thing on the mind of a nurse who has just been jailed for 20 years, it is only the UKCC who can make a decision as to whether the actions which brought that sentence warrant a charge of professional misconduct, with a view to removing that nurse from the register.

## Action points

* Consider the relationship between professional accountability and accountability to individuals and society through the law courts. Which has most relevance to your practice?

* With reference to Chapter 3, could a ruling against a nurse, in either a civil or crown court, ever be considered **not** to be an issue of professional misconduct?

* Having read the case studies in Part II, which of these could have lead to civil or criminal proceedings against the practice nurse concerned?

* Crossley (1990) believes that 'professional self-confidence' should be to the fore, rather than some notion of 'required cover', and that nurses generally only get sued because of 'indefensible incompetence' not because of minor errors of judgment. Do you consider this to be a valid statement?

# Key texts

Dimond B (1990) *Legal Aspects of Nursing*. Prentice Hall, New York

Young A (1991) *Law and Professional Conduct in Nursing*. Scutari Press, London

# References

Crossley T (1993) Too scared to care. *Nursing Standard* **6**(40): 49–50

Dimond B (1989) Exercising accountability in the legal context. *Nursing Standard* **3**(50): 38–9

Dimond B (1990) *Legal Aspects of Nursing*. Prentice Hall, New York

Tingle J (1990) Accountability and the law: how it affects the nurse. *Senior Nurse* **10**(2): 8–9

Whitehouse v. Jordan [1981] 1 All ER 267

Zander M (1995) *The Police and Criminal Evidence Act 1984*. Sweet and Maxwell, London

# Further reading

Dimond B (1991) How can you avoid legal pitfalls? (Practice nurses are taking on more responsibility than they are trained for). *Practice Nurse* **4**(7): 428–9

Finch J (1989) Inside law, (Legal aspects of nursing) *Nursing Standard* **3**(31): 38–9

Finch J (1989) Inside law, (Legal aspects of nursing). *Nursing Standard* **3**(33): 18

Finch J (1989) Legal notes, (Vicarious liability). *Nursing Standard* **4**(7): 47–8

Holmes G (1991) Are you really covered? (Legal implications for the practice nurse, with special reference to liability and negligence). *Practice Nursing* **May**: 8–9

Pyne R (1993) Frameworks, (Legal aspects of practice nursing). *Practice Nursing* **September**: 14–5

Tingle JH (1989) Ethical, legal issues for nurses: further perspectives, (Ethical and legal aspects of issues such as patient advocacy and informed consent). *NATNews* **26**(1): 16–7

Tingle J (1989) The English legal system: an introduction and discussion. *NATNews* **26**(9): 25–6

Tingle J (1990) Complaints and the law, (Nurses and the legal aspects of patient complaints). *Nursing Standard* **5**(2): 44–6

Tingle J (1990) Ethics in practice, (Overlap of legal and ethical matters in nursing). *Nursing Times* **86**(48): 54–5

Tingle J (1991) Making the law, (Health care and the law, and the importance of legal awareness for nurses). *Nursing Times* **87**(31): 52–3

# Chapter 6
# Accountability in an Employment Context

## Key Issues and Concepts

- Who is an employee?
- Issues of accountability between employers and employees
- Importance of the job description and contract of employment
- Dilemmas of professional accountability as an employee

You will recall that Chapter 2 identified that the employee–employer relationship was one of the three key domains of accountability. Aside from any consideration of the professional collegiate relationship between GP and practice nurse, it is essential, in our discussion of accountability, that we focus on their relationship as employer and employed. This is particularly relevant, given some of the issues raised in Chapter 1 concerning the power imbalance which occasionally exists in the employment situation in general practice. It is this balance of power between employer and employee which can cause difficulty in exercising accountability for one's own practice. This chapter discusses the rights and responsibilities of both the employed and the employer, and the safeguards which can be put into place to ensure that this is a constructive working relationship.

## Who is an employee?

This may seem an obvious question; however, as Hodgson (1993) points out, there is no clear definition of an employee. In legal terms, the distinction is drawn between somebody who works to some form of contract for services (an employee), and someone who provides services to another on a self-employed basis. Our definitions of employee are made more complicated in that European Community (EC) legislation, detailed in the Treaty of Rome, prevails over UK law, and must be applied when there is a conflict between the two. So far as EC law is concerned, the term 'worker' is used, rather than employee, and the essential characteristics are that during a certain period the person concerned performs services for and under the direction of another, for which remuneration is received (Hodgson, 1993). In the main, this definition is interpreted in the same way as the term 'employee' is used in the UK. A detailed overview of the definitions of employee and tests of that definition in English Law can be found in *Employment Law for Nurses* (Hodgson, 1993).

For the majority of cases, the answer is obvious. If individuals are engaged in work with a set wage or salary, undertaking activities determined by the employer, at times set by that employer, and using facilities and premises provided by the employer, in such a way that they are integrated into the employer's business, then they are employees (Hodgson,

1993). Clearly the vast majority of practice nurses would fit this description and can be identified as the employees of GPs. If the practice nurse provided services directly to patients on a GP's list, deciding when and for whom the work would be done, and claimed a fee for doing so, then she/he would be classed as self-employed. Few practice nurses work in this way, as the systems in place for GPs to receive financial reimbursement for employment of ancillary staff apply primarily to nurses employed directly by the practice (Department of Health and the Welsh Office, 1990). Until these rules are changed, GPs buying services from self-employed practice nurses could be at a financial disadvantage.

## Accountability to the employer

Having established that an employee is employed to undertake specific work as determined by the employer, it is perhaps reasonable to assume that the employee is accountable for doing so in a satisfactory manner. This is indeed the case. Practice nurse employees have, first, to accept their duty of care in the practice and, secondly, to obey the lawful instructions of their employing GP. The duty of care requirement refers to the responsibility which the employee has to work to the standards recognised as normal for the average practitioner occupied in that role. A GP can therefore expect a nurse who is employed as a practice nurse to be able to do that job competently. This is usually established by the process of drawing up a job description, discussion at interview, and agreement of a contract of employment.

Although it is rare for a GP and a practice nurse to have a relationship based on a formal 'This is what I want you to do, so go off and do it' approach, there is a legal expectation that this is part of the contractual relationship between employee and employer. The decision as to whether a practice nurse obeys the instruction of the GP is based upon its reasonableness. An instruction that would result in the nurse breaking the law would not be carried out, and a request to do something that had not been agreed in either the job description or contract could lead to a reasonable refusal.

Perhaps the most delicate area, however, in the context of nurses and doctors, as employer and employee, is the extent to which nurses can refuse an instruction based on the assumption that this would cause a breach of their *Code of Professional Conduct*. In their handbook *The Philosophy and Practice of Medical Ethics*, the British Medical Association (BMA) acknowledges that while the doctor maintains overall responsibility for medical treatment, nurses are professionals in their own right and are not obliged to follow doctors' instructions if they have reason to believe they will be damaging to the health and wellbeing of the patient (BMA, 1988) As discussed in Chapter 3, the UKCC *Code of Professional Conduct* exists alongside similar codes adhered to by medical practitioners, in order to avoid this type of dispute. Doctors and nurses should be able to bring the best from their respective professional disciplines to determine the best approach to the care of any particular patient rather than get into situations of conflict.

## Accountability to the employee

Accountability is perhaps the wrong word here, although the rights which employees have could be said to lead to a form of accountability on the part of employees through employment law. Whichever way we look at it, employees have a range of rights for which the employer is largely held responsible. With certain qualifications, these can be summarised as the right to:

- A contract of employment
- An itemised pay statement
- Be a member of a trade union and/or professional organisation
- Time off for various reasons
- Receive statutory maternity pay and to return to work having had a baby
- Not to be unfairly dismissed
- Redundancy pay
- Not to be sexually or racially discriminated against.

While it is not a legal requirement, I would add to this list the provision of a job description. This partners the contract of employment, and once agreed by both parties, it gives a clear understanding of the role and responsibilities of the practice nurse employee.

## The contract of employment

Under employment law, a contract of employment exists as soon as an employee accepts the employers conditions of service by starting work, and both parties are bound by whatever was agreed around those conditions, whether this was in writing or not. However, within two months of an individual starting work, the employer is legally obliged to provide a written statement which either contains, or refers to another document containing, the following details:

- Names of employer and employee
- Date employment began
- Job title
- Hours of work
- Pay
- Holiday and holiday pay provisions
- Sick pay arrangements
- Pension arrangements
- Notice required from either party
- Grievance, disciplinary and appeals procedures.

(NB: In the past, employees working less than 16 hours a week, unless they had worked for eight hours or more a week for five years, were exempt from the right to a written contract within 13 weeks. This exemption was removed by the Trade Union Reform and Employment Act 1993).

The contract is exactly what it says it is, i.e. a formal declaration of acceptance of terms between the employer and employee. The contract needs to cover the above points at least, but it may also include references to specific aspects of the employee's work, such as whether a mileage allowance is payable if a practice nurse is expected to use his/her own car for work, and whether the practice provides additional insurance for the work-related use of that vehicle (see Case study 8, page 109).

Once a proper contract is in place, it should be relatively easy to resolve the majority of problems which could arise as a result of either party's accountability in the employment situation. It is in the best interest of practice nurse employee and GP employer to ensure that the contract accurately reflects the discussion of terms at the interview, and is signed and agreed as soon as possible. Guidelines on the content of employment contracts can be obtained from both the BMA and Royal College of Nursing (Ellis, 1994; RCN, 1995). Each of these provides draft contracts and similar advice on how to use them, so that either party — GP employer or practice nurse employee — can turn to the one with which he/she is most comfortable.

It is wise for any practice nurse who is unsure about the contract of employment being offered to have it looked over by a representative of his/her trade union/professional organisation. A reasonable employer will have no problem with this, and should consider it to be another step towards preventing future difficulties.

## The job description

This is not a legal requirement so far as employment law is concerned; however, provision of a job description can be just as important as the legal documentation. Copp (1988) indicates the useful place that job descriptions have in offsetting potential problems between employer and employee, and Hyde (1985) demonstrates the clear link between the ability to be accountable and having a proper job description. I would agree with both authors as over the years I have found that problems concerning differing perspectives on competence, who is responsible and accountable for what in the practice, training needs, pay, and a whole range of other factors are related more to the absence of a proper job description than to having a definitive contract.

First, in deciding why a practice nurse is required in the practice, the GP, and perhaps the practice manager, will have to sit down and draw up a job description to be made available to anyone enquiring about the post on offer. It is essential for any practice nurse applying for a job to at least see a draft job description so as to get an idea of what is required of him/her. Brief descriptions such as 'normal/usual practice nurse duties' should be treated with caution.

Secondly, in agreeing the job description, the employing GP will know what to expect from the practice nurse, and what the nurse has agreed she/he is able to do. This simple understanding would reduce the many problems which have come to my attention when either GPs have not realised the limitations of the nurse they have employed, or the nurse, having accepted the job, now thinks that a particular aspect of the work should not be his/her responsibility. For instance, I do not see how the situation described in Case study 4, page 83 could have arisen if the practice nurses and GP concerned had all agreed the respective job descriptions.

Thirdly, although the rate of pay is detailed in the contract, this should correlate with the nature of the work being done, particularly the responsibility inherent in that work, as detailed in the job description. This is an important point, as 99% of GPs still pay practice nurses according to the clinical grading criteria adopted in the mainstream NHS, and those criteria should directly relate to job description.

The RCN (1995) publication *Guidelines for GPs on the Employment of Nurses in General Practice* offers a series of caveats describing practice nursing work which are useful in drawing up job descriptions.

## Itemised pay statement

Simply, an employer must provide each employee with a pay statement showing gross and net pay, any deductions, and the reasons for them. Alternatively, in the case of fixed deductions, an annual statement can be provided detailing the amounts and reasons for deduction.

## Trade union membership

Although GP employers are not obliged to recognise the right of a trade union to represent their employees — although in reality many do — they cannot prevent practice nurses from belonging to a union of their choice. If the GP accepts that a union can represent members in the practice workplace, and a practice nurse is appointed as a representative of that union, then that nurse should be allowed time off with pay to carry out union duties if those duties are concerned with industrial relations between the employer and employees.

## Time off for public duties

Under certain circumstances, an employer is required to permit any employee who holds certain public positions time off to fulfil the duties of those positions. Examples would be to act as a justice of the peace, as members of certain authorities (such as health and education), and as members of statutory tribunals. However, the employer does not have to pay the employee for time taken off in this way.

(**NB**: Time off for participation in the reserved armed forces is currently being reviewed, with a proposal that employers be reimbursed for the pay of any employee away on exercise, training or active service.)

## Time off for antenatal care

If a practice nurse were to become pregnant, a GP employer cannot unreasonably refuse time off with pay to attend appointments for antenatal care. Apart from the first appointment in the pregnancy, the employer can ask to see a certificate from a doctor, midwife or health visitor, stating that the employee is pregnant, and for evidence of subsequent appointments.

## Unfair dismissal

Employees have the right not to be unfairly dismissed. Employees who think they have been unfairly dismissed may seek assistance and remedy by way of complaint to an industrial tribunal.

## Redundancy pay

If a practice nurse has been employed for at least two years, the employing GP would have to make a lump sum 'redundancy payment' by way of compensation. The amount payable is related to the age of the employee, length of service, and weekly pay. Any practice nurse in this situation is advised to contact his/her trade union representative for advice and assistance.

## Sex and race discrimination

It is unlawful for an employer to discriminate on grounds of sex or against married persons. It is also unlawful to discriminate on racial grounds, i.e. minority ethnic grouping, nationality or colour. These provisions apply to both the recruitment of new staff and the treatment of existing employees. There are **no exceptions** based on practice size.

## Equal pay

Employers are required to give equal treatment to men and women employed to do 'like work', work related as equivalent, and work of equal value. The principle is not restricted to pay, but extends to all aspects of the employment contract. Consequently, a GP could not pay a male practice nurse more than a female (or vice versa) so long as they fit the 'like work' criterion.

## Summary

Although this book concerns issues of accountability, this discussion of employment law is not out of place in that the issues raised cannot be separated from the responsibilities placed upon nursing and medicine so far as professional accountability is concerned.

As we saw in Chapter 2, there is an inextricable link between concepts of authority, the ability for self-determination, autonomy, and accountability. All of these aspects are influenced just as much by contracts of employment and job descriptions as they are by professional codes of conduct. Bearing in mind the historical overview of practice nursing in Chapter 1, it is perhaps this area of the nursing profession that is most problematic when it comes to matching accountability to one's profession to that of one's employer. Nursing and medicine operate from differing philosophical standpoints and their practitioners have been prepared in markedly different ways. In addition to affording each other the benefit of respect as colleagues and equals, it is useful to ensure that all potential areas of conflict concerning what a job entails, how it is described, and how it is remunerated are dealt with in advance rather than having difficulties arise in the middle of a busy practice with patients coming in and out.

## Action points

* *If you do not have a contract of employment or job description, use the advice in this chapter and the key texts listed below to formulate draft versions to be agreed with your employer. Seek advice from your trade union / professional organisation as needed.*

* *If you have a contract and job description, do they reflect the guidance in this chapter? If not, seek advice from your trade union/professional organisation as needed.*

* *Compare your contract and job description. How does their content allow you to be accountable for your practice?*

## Key texts

Ellis N (1994) *Employing Staff*. British Medical Association, London

Hodgson J (1993) *Employment Law for Nurses*. Quay Books, Dinton, Nr Salisbury

Royal College of Nursing (1995) *Guidance on the Employment of Nurses in General Practice*. RCN, London

## References

British Medical Association (1988) *The Philosophy and Practice of Medical Ethics*. British Medical Association, London: 67

Copp G (1988) Professional accountability: the conflict. *Nursing Times and Nursing Mirror* **84**(43): 42–4

Department of Health and the Welsh Office (1990) *Terms and Conditions for Doctors in General Practice. NHS (General Medical and Pharmaceutical Services) Regulations 1974 Schedules 1–3 Amended*. HMSO, London

Ellis N (1994) *Employing Staff*. British Medical Association, London

Hodgson J (1993) *Employment Law for Nurses*. Quay Books, Dinton, Nr Salisbury: 3

Hyde P (1985) Accountability. *Nursing Mirror* **160**(16): 24–5

Royal College of Nursing (1995) *Guidelines for GPs on the Employment of Nurses in General Practice*. RCN, London

## Further reading:

Aikin O (1992) The morass of maternity law, (EC developments and the rights of employees during and after pregnancy). *Personnel Management* **24**(3): 25,27

Dimond B (1991) All part of the job, (Legal problems of incorporating the UKCC code of conduct within employment contracts). *Nursing Times* **87**(33): 44–6

Finch J (1989) Legal notes, (Additional liability of employers for employees' wrongdoings). *Nursing Standard* **4**(4): 47–8

Goldman L (1994) A whistlestop tour of TURERA, (Trade Union Reform and Employment Rights Act 1993). *Occupational Health* **46**(2): 59–60

Howard G (1994) The new maternity rights, (Implications of the Trade Union Reform and Employment Rights Act 1993 for pregnant employees). *Occupational Health* **46**(4): 133–4

Nazarko L (1992) A woman's rightful place (Working women and child care). *Nursing Standard* **6**(33): 46–7

# Part II
# Case Studies

*'One may discuss values and professional accountability forever; it is interesting, informative and stimulating. But sooner or later abstract principles must be applied to real situations, and nurses, being pragmatic people, will want to know where the various abstract moral principles fit into the scheme of daily activities.'*

(Fromer, 1981)

With these sentiments in mind, in Part II of the book we move on from a theoretical analysis of accountability to apply that theory to the reality of practice. Many practice nurses contact the Royal College of Nursing (RCN) for advice concerning aspects of their work, which may have ethical, legal and, of course, professional implications. The case studies described in this section are drawn from the real experience of practice nurses who have received assistance from the RCN and are intended to provide some examples of situations facing practice nurses and to describe how they were dealt with.

All of the case studies are real, and are an account of one incident or several which have been combined. Additionally, I may have used a little 'poetic licence' in setting the scene for each study, but the content remains an accurate depiction of what happened. All the practice nurses involved in these incidents have freely given their permission for the examples to be used, although their names and those of the patients have been changed for obvious reasons. Any similarity between the names used and those of actual individuals is purely coincidental.

We should also point out that the subject matter of some of the case studies is exceptional, and is in no way intended to suggest that the practice described can be found elsewhere. However, these events did happen, and it is from them that we can learn to avoid difficulties in the future, no matter how great the odds may be against their recurrence.

In the discussion following each case study, reference to the standard texts mentioned in Part I of the book is taken as granted, in particular the *Code of Professional Conduct*, and *The Scope of Professional Practice*. Where reference to other material should be made, this is indicated at the end of each case study.

Once you have read a case study, apply the theory from Part I of the book and see how it fits the situation described. Consider what the view of either the UKCC's Professional Conduct Committee or Health Committee, or a civil or criminal court, might have been of the actions of the practice nurse concerned. Finally, give some thought as to whether the type of situation described could ever happen in your practice.

# Reference

Fromer MJ (1981) *Ethical Issues in Health Care.* C V Mosby, St Louis

# Case Study 1
# Practice Nurse Mary Ellis

## Key Issues and Concepts:

- Informed Consent
- Record Keeping
- The use of Protocols

Mustafa Ali is a 44-year-old Egyptian man with a limited understanding of English. He has been registered with the practice for several years, although his attendance is infrequent as he returns to his native Egypt for long trips, often lasting many months.

Today, Mr Ali is attending the routine Monday clinic for travel vaccinations before another trip to Egypt. Practice nurse Mary Ellis is running the clinic. She knows Mr Ali from old and remembers giving him travel vaccinations before, as indeed is indicated in his notes.

The practice has a standard protocol for travel vaccinations which Mary has used many times before and is using today. Mary works her way through the protocol and eventually gets around to administering the vaccinations.

Mustafa's shirt is quite tight in the sleeves and Mary suggests that he removes it to make things a little easier. As he removes his shirt, Mary notices several bruises on his chest. She had never seen bruises like this before and asks Mustafa what has happened. Mustafa makes light of the situation, and laughingly recounts that he had had a little too much to drink a couple of days ago and fell over a chair, banging his chest. Through a combination of broken English and sign language, Mustafa assures Mary that he has not hurt himself seriously and that he is in good health. Apart from the bruises Mary can see, Mustafa does appear quite healthy. He is a little thin, but then he had always been like that. Mary Ellis gives Mr Ali his vaccinations, wishes him well on his trip and calls in the next patient.

At the end of a long week, practice nurse Mary Ellis was looking forward to her weekend off, but just then the senior partner to the practice, Dr Draper, appeared looking rather worried and asked to speak to her in his office.

Dr Draper had just received a telephone call from the police. It seems that an Egyptian gentleman, by the name of Mustafa Ali, had died in mysterious circumstances in mid-flight on an Egyptian airliner on Monday afternoon, and had been traced to the practice through the vaccination record card in his pocket. The death had happened close to Egypt, and the authorities there had taken the matter into their hands, recording an open verdict and allowing Mr Ali's family to bury him. However, the police had also found on Mr Ali an appointment card for the outpatients clinic of a private London Hospital and also made enquiries there.

## Outcome

It was revealed that Mustafa had been under the treatment of a leading specialist for a rare form of cancer which had been deemed incurable. He had recently received a course of cytotoxic therapy and was now being maintained on pain control only. The specialist confirmed that Mr Ali had chosen to return home to die.

It would seem, then, that even though Mustafa knew he was dying and was booked onto a plane that afternoon, he had followed his usual practice of attending for his travel vaccinations. The strange bruising which Mary Ellis had not recognised was a sign of his carcinoma, and in his immunocompromised state the vaccinations she had administered may well have led to his death, but who knows?

Mary Ellis was sure, however, that she had killed one of her patients and that it was all her fault. But was it?

## Discussion

Much as Mary Ellis was blaming herself for contributing to Mr Ali's death, there is little she could have done to avert the situation. The practice had a comprehensive protocol for travel vaccinations and she had followed it to the letter. She had checked Mr Ali's blood pressure, pulse and temperature, all of which were fine, and he had told her he was feeling very well. He had given no indication that he was flying to Egypt almost as soon as he had had his vaccinations, and he never mentioned his serious illness of which the strange chest bruising was the only outward manifestation.

Mary had sought to establish whether Mr Ali was in good health, her observations confirmed that he was, and so did Mr Ali himself, but he had lied — he was going home to die. Mary had gained Mustafa's consent, she had explained the vaccinations as she always did, and Mustafa had seemed to understand. What else could she have done?

Unfortunately for Mary she was faced with a patient who had come to terms with his death or had at least closed his mind to his condition, yet presented as normal for his vaccinations. For whatever reason, he chose not to discuss his true health status with her. But there were the bruises. Mary could have persisted in her questioning concerning their origin. Did they look as if they were caused by a fall a couple of days ago? Maybe he wouldn't mind if the doctor had a quick look also? Even so, would Dr Draper have done any different from his practice nurse?

Maybe the language barrier had been a problem. Although Mary and Mustafa had managed to communicate on a basic level, had his limited understanding of English restricted the way in which Mary could have used her negotiating and counselling skills to find out a little more about his injuries when he simply laughed them off as the result of a drunken stumble?

If Mustafa had been attending the surgery for more than a travel vaccination, it would probably have been wise to try to arrange for some form of interpretation to be available, but Mary had not felt that this was necessary in the case of a routine travel vaccination.

It is impossible to lay the blame for Mustapha's death on Mary. His body is in Egypt and he was buried without a postmortem; his cancer could have killed him on the plane just as well as anything else.

To put it simply, Mary had followed all the correct procedures, yet her patient misled her at best and lied to her at worst. She could have pursued the cause of the bruises further, but she did her best in the circumstances, and it is the balance of probability that any other practice nurse would have done the same (consider the test for negligence outlined in Chapter 5). Other aspects in Mary's favour were the fact that her practice had detailed protocols which could be shown as evidence of the procedures which would be routinely followed in the practice. Tingle (1992) points out that such documentation is particularly important in that it forms a 'statement of intent'. That is to say that a court of law would look favourably on the existence of a protocol as being evidence of the usual way of carrying out a particular activity in the practice. Mary also kept detailed records of her interventions with patients. All in all, this practice nurse's work was thorough, systematic and well documented.

All Mary has to live with now are her own feelings of guilt. For several months she could not give any form of vaccination, and she knew herself that she was putting her patients through a Spanish Inquisition style of questioning before she would let them out of the surgery door.

Mary has received professional counselling enabling her to stay in her job as a practice nurse; after all, she was good at her job. Why should she be driven from it by an unforeseen, unfortunate incident that was not of her making?

# References

Tingle J (1992) Legal implications of standard setting in nursing. *Br J Nursing* **1**(5): 728–31

UKCC (1992) *Standards for the Administration of Medicines*. UKCC, London

UKCC (1993) *Standards for Records and Record Keeping*. UKCC, London

# Further reading

Cowan V (1987) Documentation, (Legal aspects). *Nursing* **3**(14): 527–9

Dimond B (1989) Practice nursing and the law, Consent to treatment 1. *Practice Nurse* **1**(8): 342–4

Dimond B (1989) Consent to treatment 2. *Practice Nurse* **1**(9): 391–2

Finch J (1989) Inside law, (Law on duties of care and consent to treatment). *Nursing Standard* **3**(46): 52–3

Morton WJ (1987) The doctrine of informed consent. *Medicine and The Law* **6**(2): 117–25

Parker S (1992) Administering medicine, (Legal aspects for nurses). *Practice Nursing* **October**: 8

Parker S (1992) Seeking consent, (Patient consent, with reference to the practice nurse). *Practice Nursing* **September**: 27

Pinfold C (1991) Patient consent and the law. *Hospital Management International*: 115–7

Sorrell JM (1991) Effects of writing/speaking on comprehension of information for informed consent, (Patient understanding). *W J Nursing Res* **13**(1): 110–22

Tingle J (1990) Patient consent: the issues, (Legal implications for nurses). *Nursing Standard* **5**(9): 52–4

# Case Study 2.
# Practice Nurse Millie Gordon

## Key Issues and Concepts:

- Duty of care
- Competence to practice
- Negligence

Gemima Andrews was playing in the courtyard of the small block of flats in which she lived. She was a cheerful six year old, although recently she had found it a little hard to keep smiling as the other children had been making fun of the blotchy skin on her face.

Today was no exception, and before long Gemima had run into her home crying. Her mother, Ann, consoled her and thought to herself that she really must find out what was wrong with her daughter. She knew it would be difficult to get an appointment with the GP today 'but, of course,' she thought to herself, 'I'll ask Millie what she thinks when she comes home from work this evening.'

Millie Gordon lived a little way down the landing to Gemima and Ann Andrews, and was well known to most of the families living in the flats. She had lived there for 15 years now, after moving in when she started her nurse training at the large teaching hospital nearby. She had left the hospital two years ago to take up a post as a practice nurse locally.

Millie had had a hard day at the practice when she finally got in, but she was glad to be home and put the dinner on. There was a good film on the television tonight and she was looking forward to a quiet night in. By the time Ann Andrews called around with Gemima, she was just about to serve up her food; she had timed it just right to sit down as the opening credits rolled for her film.

Millie knew Ann and Gemima quite well. They were not registered with any of the partners she worked for, but were on the list of a single-handed GP not too far away. Ann explained that Gemima had developed these 'blotches' on her face over the last couple of months and they just didn't seem to be going away. Millie agreed that Gemima's face did look a little strange, although she hadn't really noticed when she had waved to her across the courtyard a number of times recently.

Millie questioned Gemima's mother as to whether she had changed soap powders recently, or had bought Gemima any new clothes, or whether Gemima had managed to convince her to get her a kitten at last. Millie's speculation centred around something she had remembered about allergies causing the sort of blotchiness that Gemima now had.

Millie was pretty sure that it was an allergy to something. She suggested that Ann should wash Gemima's clothes in a non-biological detergent, and use plain soap to wash. She could hear the action hotting up in the background — both in the oven and on the film — and hoped that Ann would be satisfied now.

Indeed she was and Ann thanked Millie for her trouble. Gemima kissed Millie goodbye and Millie settled down to that nice quiet night in.

## Outcome

A couple of weeks passed. Millie Gordon had decided that she needed a break from work and had taken some time off to go on a cheap off-season holiday abroad with a colleague. Gemima Andrews' face got steadily worse, and as Millie wasn't around, Ann finally resolved to take her to the doctor.

When she saw the doctor, Ann was quite surprised at his urgent attention. She though he was a good doctor although he was a bit slow sometimes. On this occasion, however, Dr Bemali was insistent that Gemima should be seen by a skin specialist at the hospital without delay. He actually rang the hospital while they were there and told the specialist they would be around that afternoon.

Ann and Gemima arrived in outpatients. There was a bit of a fuss as the doctor they had come to see wasn't running a clinic today and nobody had told the receptionist that they were coming. Eventually Dr Simmons, the consultant dermatologist, arrived. After some time he rang another colleague to ask for help with Gemima. After the other doctor — he called himself an oncologist — had seen Gemima, Ann was told that they would have to admit her to hospital immediately for treatment.

The medical staff were very good and carefully explained to Ann Andrews that the skin cancer her daughter had was very rare, and there was nothing she or anyone else could have done to prevent it. Gemima had several courses of chemotherapy but eventually died only four months after she had been admitted to hospital.

The Andrews family were not surprisingly very upset and very angry. Who was to blame for this? Millie had said it was only an allergy and that it would get better. Millie!

The Andrews family sought legal assistance, and eventually Millie Gordon, practice nurse, received a court summons resulting from a private prosecution they were bringing. The charge was negligence. Essentially they were asserting that Millie had given advice about Gemima's face which had led Ann Andrews to believe that her condition was not serious. This belief led her to think it wasn't worth going to see the doctor and so she didn't — until it was too late.

As it happened, on considering the testimony of the hospital medical staff, the solicitor acting for the Andrews family advised them that it was bound to exonerate Millie. The doctors' opinion was that even if Ann Andrews had sought immediate medical attention for her daughter, the prognosis would have been extremely poor. The 'authorities' had felt that there were no suspicious circumstances around Gemima's unfortunate death, and now Millie Gordon was likely to walk free from the court as there was no case which could be proven against her. The family took the advice of their solicitor and dropped the case.

# Discussion

What did practice nurse Millie Gordon do wrong ? She had given advice to a friend and a neighbour which she believed to be true. She wasn't at work and so she didn't have to keep notes or refer her to the GP or anything, but now her friend had just attempted to wreck her career through a court case.

In fact, Millie overstepped the mark as far as one of the most basic principles of nursing practice is concerned — knowing the boundaries of one's own competence. It didn't matter that Millie was not at work; she was a nurse, registered with the UKCC, a body which charged her to adhere to her professional code of conduct at all times, not just during the hours she happened to be in paid employment as a practice nurse. This adherence includes the fact that a nurse must acknowledge the limits of his/her own competence and not exceed those limits.

When Ann and Gemima Andrews stood on the doorstep, rushed as she may have been by her dinner boiling over and the film about to begin, Millie should have stopped to think whether she was sufficiently competent to give the advice she gave. At the very least she should have told Ann that even if the blotches didn't look too bad, she must go to see her GP. Had Millie gone to work in general practice from a position in a dermatology or oncology unit, she may have been better placed to advise Ann, but even then she should have directed her towards a medical practitioner whose job it would have been to diagnose or refer on as appropriate.

Millie Gordon was quite lucky really. There was no real case for her to answer in court, as her advice, proper or otherwise, would have had little bearing on the outcome. Her situation was not considered by the UKCC, and she still has a job today.

The case of Gemima Andrews was a little extreme, and questions could certainly be asked about the responsibilities of others to seek assistance — her mother for example. But as extreme as it may be, nurses face similar situations every day. How many times have you been asked for advice because you are known to be a nurse? And how many times have you given what you believe to be constructive advice, because, like Millie, you think you remember reading something about it somewhere?

Millie's case was in a hurried situation at home, but have you ever been in a rush at the surgery when all the GPs are out on their rounds and the receptionist asks if you would just take a look at so and so who is getting upset in the waiting area. Are you certain that you know how far to go in these circumstances as far as your role as a nurse and not a doctor is concerned? Think about it.

There is no need to barricade your front door when you get home and not speak to anyone about anything remotely concerning their health, or to be totally inflexible at work. But take time to consider whether you do know what you are talking about — and remember Millie Gordon.

# Further reading:

Edler CR (1986) If a friend asks you for medical advice, (Nurse giving informal medical advice). RN August: 38–40

# Case Study 3
# Practice Nurse Katy Marsh.

## Key Issues and Concepts:

- Consent

- Record Keeping

- Negligence

Katy Marsh was driving back towards the practice following a busy morning of home visits, mainly to perform over-75 health checks and give the odd flu jab. She wondered whether she would beat the partners back in from their rounds and have to do the washing-up from the team meeting earlier in the day. She smiled to herself remembering Dr Jameson's confession that, while he had agreed to take his place as a mug scrubber if in first, he had made a particular effort to do a 'social visit' on an elderly patient last week to avoid this onerous duty. 'Anyway, enough of this daydreaming,' thought Katy, 'concentrate on the road and back to the surgery.'

While Katy and her GP colleagues were out that morning, patients had still called in at the surgery, mostly to pick up repeat prescriptions and some to make routine appointments. One visitor had been a particularly anxious schoolteacher, Susan Gill.

Susan had called into the practice just as all the partners and Katy Marsh had left to do their house calls. She was just under three months pregnant, or so she thought, and the cause of her distress was that on coming into school that morning she had found that two pupils in her infants' class — the Robinson twins — were off school with German measles.

Only yesterday had she been talking to the school nurse about the benefits of rubella vaccination programmes, and how German measles can cause serious problems for babies as they develop in the womb. Now she knew for certain that she had been in contact with at least two carriers of the rubella virus, and she had rushed straight round to the practice for some advice and guidance.

Unfortunately for Susan Gill there was only the practice manager and the two receptionists available to allay her anxieties. They actually did this rather well and assured Susan that she could see the practice nurse as soon as she got in from her visits, which shouldn't be long now. However, Susan told the receptionist that she had calmed down a bit now, and thought she had better get back to school. Could she possibly get an appointment after lunch? This was agreed, and Susan Gill was to be 'slotted in' to see Katy Marsh before she began her immunisation clinic that afternoon. The receptionist made a note in the 'nurse's book' behind the counter: 'Susan Gill — schoolteacher — ? rubella'.

Katy was right; Dr Jameson and the other partners had managed to stay out just long enough for her to have to do the washing-up. Anyway, she still had time to write up the morning's visits and grab a sandwich before her afternoon clinic started. Just then the receptionist popped her head around the door to give Katy the 'nurse's book'.

Katy groaned and wearily opened the book. It was always full of notes of things to be done at the last minute, and details of patients who had just called in and managed to persuade the receptionist to 'just squeeze them in' to her already busy schedule. Today was no exception: here's one — Susan Gill, schoolteacher, edged in before her first appointment.

## Outcome

As Katy marvelled at her skill in fitting her seemingly 100 hours a week's worth of patients into her 40-hour week, the buzzer on the office wall sounded and a second later Susan Gill was at the door. Katy hurriedly swallowed her last mouthful of cheese sandwich, brushed the crumbs off her desk and invited Susan in. 'Ah yes — Susan Gill — rubella,' Katy greeted Susan. She asked Susan to sit down and began to draw up the vaccine. 'You called this morning about rubella?' enquired Katy, 'Yes,' came the nervous reply. 'This won't hurt a bit,' Katy assured her as she proficiently administered the rubella vaccination. As Susan Gill patted her stomach and expressed relief at the fact that her baby would now be safe, the blood began to drain from Katy Marsh's face as she put two and two together.

If you weren't there already, you can guess the story from here on. A worried Susan Gill had called back to discuss her fears with Katy, and now those fears had most certainly been realised. Not only had she been in contact with children bearing the rubella virus, but it had actually been injected into her bloodstream.

Susan Gill was beside herself as Katy stumbled her way through the explanation of her dreadful mistake. Dr. Jameson saw her in an effort to explain the consequences, but Susan was distraught and was already demanding an abortion. She eventually fled the practice in tears.

## Discussion

Although there is no evidence to suggest certain damage to a fetus from the administration of rubella vaccine to a pregnant women, Susan Gill took no chances and had her pregnancy terminated at around 12 weeks.

Surprising as it may seem, she came to see herself as the victim of an unfortunate accident, and even blamed herself for rushing round to the practice and not making a proper appointment for the evening surgery. She took no action against the partners, nor — perhaps even more surprisingly — against Katy Marsh. Somewhat ironically, soon after the incident Susan moved out of the area as her partner had been offered a lucrative contract with the marketing division of a large vaccine manufacturer in another part of the country.

Katy Marsh had a lot more difficulty in resolving this matter as an accident, although having traced back through the events of that fateful day she could easily see why it had happened.

The practice thoroughly reviewed its appointment system and the way in which messages were left, and Katy's workload was eased by the employment of another practice nurse on a part-time basis. Hopefully such a dreadful mistake would never happen again.

Maybe Katy Marsh was the victim of an unfortunate string of circumstances. The practice in which she worked did have a reasonable communication system, regular practice meetings were held, and patients and problems in the practice were thoroughly discussed. But, at a lower level, things could have been a lot better — the 'nurse's book' for instance.

Katy Marsh had had a busy morning, her mind was set on running an afternoon clinic set aside for vaccination/immunisation, and the entry in the book was ambiguous: 'Susan Gill — schoolteacher —? rubella'. The receptionist had intended to convey that Susan had a query about rubella, namely her contact with the schoolchildren while pregnant, but what Katy saw was an indication that somebody had been squeezed in to have a rubella vaccination.

What about ascertaining 'informed consent' from the patient? Katy asked Susan Gill a leading question — 'You came about rubella?' — and heard the answer she wanted to hear, i.e. that Susan was asking for vaccination. It could be argued that Susan Gill should have been more explicit, but the onus was certainly on Katy to be sure in her mind that her patient was fully consenting to the vaccination she was about to give. Why should Susan Gill not have believed that some new form of jab had been developed to counteract the effects of her being in contact with those children — she was a teacher, not a practice nurse or a doctor.

The UKCC is very specific in identifying the responsibility of nurses when it comes to obtaining consent in a situation such as this:

> '*It is not safe to assume that the patient or client has enough knowledge, even about basic treatment, for them to make an informed choice without an explanation (UKCC, 1996)*'

and:

> '*...you are often best placed to know about the emotions, concerns and views of the patient or client and so be able to judge the type of information the patient or client needs and make sure that it is understood (UKCC, 1996)*'

Clearly, if Katy Marsh had followed this advice, then the tragic circumstances of this incident would have been avoided. The practice even had a comprehensive protocol for vaccination and immunisations, yet Katy was in a rush, her mind was distracted, and she did not follow it.

Katy Marsh had allowed her workload to increase to an extent where she had no time to think or prepare herself between different activities. She had a busy morning, a rushed lunch break, and was irritated at having patients squeezed into her busy schedule. As a means of communication, the 'nurse's book' was a disaster. It would have been better if the receptionist had written out fully what Susan Gill had come in for earlier, but that still would not have been an excuse for Katy to skimp so badly on her interaction with the patient.

Again, this example seems dramatic, and in the 'it could never happen to me' category. But even the most improbable mistakes can happen when you are overworked and stressed, and circumstances like the poor communication system in this practice can combine to produce a fateful mix which rapidly turns the odds against you.

## Reference

UKCC (1992) *Standards for the Administration of Medicines*. UKCC, London
UKCC (1993) *Standards for Records and Record Keeping*. UKCC, London
UKCC (1996) *Ethical Guidelines for Professional Practice*. UKCC, London

## Further reading

As for case study 1.

# Case Study 4
# Practice Nurses Sue Garth, Beth Willis, Meg Brooks and Lynn Taylor.

## Key Issues and Concepts:

- Expanded roles
- Competence to practice
- Delegation
- Employment rights

Sue, Beth, Meg and Lynn were good friends working for a large seven-partner practice in the North of England. Lynn had only just joined the practice, but already knew the others very well as she had been working as a district nurse visiting patients on the surgery list for many years. Sue was the old stager of the team — as she called herself. She had worked for Dr Rogers, the senior partner, for 12 years, long before they moved into the new Lakeside Surgery premises just before the new GP Contract came in a year ago. Beth had been with the practice three years, and Meg a little over two years.

This morning was no exception to the rule: the four of them had been working flat out running two of the practice's main clinic sessions, one for diabetes and the other for asthma. These clinics were very successful and always busy; in fact, Sue remarked that the four of them could probably be kept busy running them and nothing else, with a series of repeats throughout the week.

Although they had had a busy morning, they would get a rest later on as it was the day of the practice team meeting, and they generally had the chance to let their minds drift off while the practice manger spouted on about costs and efficiency, minimising waste, and all the rest of it. However, although they didn't know it, today's meeting was to be the start of a harrowing time for the four friends.

The meeting did start with a boring lecture from the practice manager — no suprises there, and then Dr Rogers cleared his throat and announced that they were going to bring a new and exciting initiative to the practice. It would seem that the Lakeside GPs had been particularly impressed with a conference they had attended the previous week concerning women's health. They subsequently agreed that in addition to providing the basic cervical screening service, as they already did, the practice was going to start running a well-women clinic which would require (like most things in the practice) total commitment from all the practice nurses.

Lynn Taylor was particularly interested in this idea, as she had not had much involvement with women's health, having just left her job as a district nurse. She was keen to do smears and whatever, just like her colleagues did at the moment. But, as the meeting progressed, the total commitment required from all the practice nurses rapidly became translated into boosting cervical smear rates at all costs. It would seem that in addition to attending their conference, the partners had been spurred into action by the practice manager's prediction that they were not even going to hit the lower target for their practice population.

In fact, the partners were so keen to get going on this new initiative that well-women clinics were to begin the week after next. There was a bank holiday in between, so everyone would be able to steel themselves for the onslaught — all hands to the Cervex brushes.

The four practice nurses stayed in the room as the partners and practice managers left. The discussion ranged from the implications of squeezing in more clinic sessions, to the interest in developing something new. Beth was particularly keen to set up a well-women clinic as she didn't think they gave a particularly good service just now; all they really did was invite patients in, take a smear and say goodbye. At this point Lynn made her first expression of doubt: 'But isn't that just what the partners want us to carry on doing — but more of it? And anyway, I don't even know how to take a smear — how am I going to learn in time?'

Sue reassured Lynn. She told her that Dr Rogers had taught all of them to do smears, and would also show her. Far from reassuring Lynn, this troubled her. Part of her interest in setting up the well-women clinic stemmed from the comments she had received from patients after Dr Rogers had done their smears. He seemed to have little time and was abrupt, and she had seen with her own eyes while chaperoning that he was rough and tended to treat women like a slab of meat. She didn't want to learn from him. 'Can't you teach me?' she asked Sue. 'After all you have been doing it for years?' 'No,' said Sue, 'Dr. Rogers is the expert; he will teach you and then you will take the smears.'

Lynn's concerns did not go away, and the next day, on her morning off, she telephoned the RCN to discuss her position. She learned that it was her responsibility to ensure that she was competent to take on this new role in women's health screening, and that until she was sure she could deliver this care to a proper standard she should be wary of taking on the role. On the advice of the RCN, Lynn contacted her FHSA facilitator and found out that the FHSA was going to run a short course on women's health, including how to take a smear — her worries were over. Lynn resolved to discuss this with Dr Rogers that afternoon.

## Outcome

Lynn had the meeting and her hopes were dashed. Far from welcoming her suggestion that she should go on the course and become a real expert for when the well-women clinic started, Dr Rogers went — well — potty. **He** was the expert and he was quite able to train a practice nurse to take a *** smear! Unfortunately he did swear, and before Lynn could recover from the shock he told her in no uncertain terms that if she persisted in her silly ideas he would have to find another nurse who would fit in with his methods.

Lynn protested that the RCN had told her that she must decide whether she is competent, and she felt that the best way of doing this was to attend the FHSA course —

more swearing! Lynn really couldn't believe what she was hearing (neither could Sue, Beth and Meg who were now huddled outside the door). Lynn persisted with her final pitch that she would rather learn how to do a smear in the general context of women's health (she had read that somewhere), and she would rather learn from another nurse. That was it; Dr Rogers' door swung open, the other practice nurses scattered and Lynn emerged tears streaming down her face. She had been sacked.

Sue Garth remonstrated with her boss of 12 years, but he was having none of it — she could go to as well if she liked.

Lynn wasn't going to take her dismissal lying down, and Sue, Beth and Meg were very supportive, if a little concerned about their own position. They decided, first, to get in touch with their FHSA facilitator and arranged to see her.

After work that day, the four practice nurses met in the facilitator's office and told the tale. The facilitator listened as Lynn described how her intentions to become a competent practitioner had landed her in such hot water; she hadn't intended to upset Dr Rogers, but she really believed should could learn more from the FHSA course than from him. The other nurses were uneasy as Lynn produced her *Code of Professional Conduct* booklet from her handbag: 'I was only going by this,' she insisted, 'and the RCN said I was right!'

The four nurses and the facilitator talked about the situation in the practice, their work in the clinics, and in particular about women's health and cervical smears. Eventually, Lynn's colleagues, even old stager Sue, admitted that they had not been too happy at learning from Dr Rogers. He knew how to do a smear all right, but his manner left much to be desired — he was certainly no nurse. Even Lynn found herself laughing at this.

The upshot was that the facilitator talked through the situation with her medical adviser colleague. Subsequently, there took place the noisiest, most abusive, yet most constructive team meeting in the history of the Lakeside practice. The facilitator came along, and with the practice nurses went through the events leading up to Lynn's dismissal.

GPs and nurses eventually agreed that they would take up the facilitator's offer of assistance in setting up the well-women clinic. The FHSA would not breathe down the practice's neck over the smear targets, and Lynn and Meg would attend the FHSA-run course.

Dr Rogers emphasised the pressure he was under in making the new surgery pay, and the other partners agreed that just like the practice nurses they were working flat out and it was hard to stop and think clearly. Dr Rogers eventually admitted that even though Sue Garth had worked for him for 12 years, he had never really got to grips with what she actually did, but he did know that other practices had taken on more nurses at the time of the new Contract and found them to be of great assistance. He now saw the need to use his medical skills, and those of his colleagues, in tandem with the skills of the practice nurses to deliver a high quality package of care.

These revelations did not of course happen overnight, but Lynn did get an apology and her job back, and the Lakeside Practice moved forwards into a new era of teamworking and collaboration, from which no doubt many patients now benefit.

## Discussion

There is little more to be said really. Within the team of practice nurses at Lakeside, there was a wide range of experience and longevity of service. Sue Garth in particular, had got used to Dr Rogers and his ways, and Beth Willis and Meg Brooks had settled into the system, beavering away at their clinic sessions.

It took the arrival of Lynn Taylor, who was new to the job and had gone out of her way to check up on her position so far as professional accountability was concerned, to challenge the status quo.

Lynn was right to insist on obeying clause 4 of her professional code:

*'...acknowledge any limitations in your knowledge and competence and decline any duties or responsibilities unless able to perform them in a safe and skilled manner.'*

(UKCC, 1992)

and to determine for herself the best way to achieve competency in the taking of a cervical smear. Maybe she could have been a little more tactful in challenging Dr Rogers' self-perceived position as the expert, but equally he should have respected her position as an individually accountable practitioner in her own right. Sacking her as a response to the challenge was clearly wrong, and although Lynn had been employed for a short length of time, advantage could have been taken of the circumstances of her dismissal, if not through employment legislation, then certainly through the FHSA, and maybe even Dr Rogers' own professional body, the General Medical Council.

In addition to emphasising the need for proper communication between practice team members, and an understanding of each other's roles, responsibilities and methods of practice, this case emphasises the fundamental problem facing new practice nurses who in the main do not have access to other nurses who are able to train them in aspects of their role, and have to make do with what is available, judging their own competency from a hazy reference point.

# References

UKCC (1992) *The Scope of Professional Practice*. UKCC, London

# Further reading

Gaut DA (1986) Evaluating caring competencies in nursing practice. *Topics in Clinical Nursing* **8**(2): 77–83

Girot EA (1993) Assessment of competence in clinical practice — a review of the literature. *Nurse Education Today* **13**(2): 83–90

Gorvet T (1990) Delegating to a practice nurse. *Practice Nurse* **3**(4): 24

Hohlock MA, Hohlock F (1988) Competencies for nursing practice. (Short research report) *Nursing Times and Nursing Mirror* **84**(7): 58

Luft S (1993) Competency, (With special reference to the practice nurse). *Practice Nursing* **20**: 21–2

# Case Study 5
# Practice Nurse Susan Moor

## Key Issues and Concepts:

- Confidentiality
- Informed consent and children

Susan Moor slumped into her car with a sigh — she must be mad, she thought to herself. Not only is she trying to and bring up a family of three (not including the husband) but she has also just allowed the school governors to elect her as their Chair.

As she drove out of the school car park she thought what her husband would say; he has told her before to keep quiet when volunteers are being asked for. Well, that's too bad; she had become a governor in the first place as parents had been concerned at the apparent downward trend in standards of behaviour of children in the area, and she felt it only right to do her bit. After all, her own 15-year-old daughter Claire was already suffering from the effects of the previously poor discipline at the school, and now with the new Head and opted-out status there was every opportunity for improvement. Anyway, concentrate on the road and hurry home; it is already 11.00 pm, and there is an early start to another busy day at the surgery tomorrow.

How right she had been. Susan wished she had got to bed earlier. This morning's family planning clinic had been so busy; there was just time for a quick coffee. Then the telephone rang. Meg, the receptionist, sounded a little flustered. She told Susan there was a grown man at the desk in tears; he wasn't registered but he was desperate to see the nurse. Meg knew she was at coffee, but '...Send him down,' Susan replied.

There was a knock at the door and the man burst in. He was indeed sobbing: 'I really must tell someone, I really must,' he said. Susan got him to sit down and handed over the coffee she had not had time to start, and with a snivelled thank you the man told her his name — Alan Salt — and proceeded to tell his tale.

Alan was a barman at one of the clubs in the town. Apparently he had got to know one of the customers there quite well — very well in fact — he had been sleeping with her for around six months now. However, he had just found out she was pregnant, and thought that Susan could help at her family planning clinic. Susan was about to launch into her usual discussion of options, maybe encouraging Alan to bring his partner along for a chat also, when Alan blurted out: 'for God sake, she told me last night that she is only 14; what should I do?'

What should he do indeed, thought Susan. This was a criminal offence; should the police know? But what about her Code of Conduct — she should maintain confidentiality in order to protect her client. But who is the client — Alan or his girlfriend? She decided that she must calm Alan down and get him to bring his girlfriend in to see her, and then she would go from there. She asked Alan what the girl's name was, just for the record. 'Alison Smart,' he replied. 'She goes to Greencross School.' 'Oh, right,' Susan replied, a slight quiver in her voice.

Alan Salt had gone and Susan now had time to take in what he had said. Greencross School was her school and Alison Smart was in her daughter's class. She wasn't a friend of Claire's, although she knew of her as Claire often complained that she never did any work but always got good marks — Alison Smarty Pants Smart lived up to her name, although not on this occasion thought Susan.

Lunch time came, and Susan was increasingly disturbed by what she had heard. 'I knew that school was a bad influence,' she thought, and so decided to go up there to see if she could have a chat with Alison about all of this.

When she got to the school, she found Mr Stevenson, Claire and Alison Smart's form teacher. He commented on how worried she looked and asked her what the problem was. Before she knew it, Susan was recounting the morning's events to the teacher, who like her was horrified that such a thing could happen at the school. 'It wasn't exactly at school, though, was it?' Susan remarked. Mr.Stevenson agreed, but nevertheless this would reflect on the school.

As it happened, Alison Smart and her form were out on a geography field trip all day (of course, Susan remembered, Claire had mentioned it; what was wrong with her today?) Anyway, Susan found her talk with Mr Stevenson useful, like her he was concerned for the image of the school and that the children should not be under any bad influence. She made her way back to the surgery.

Later that afternoon, Claire and Alison's form got back to school, and the path of fate continued on its way as Alison sought out Mr Stevenson to have a moan about her classmates calling her names; they had been at it all the way back in the coach. Mr Stevenson wasn't really listening to what she was saying and confronted Alison about her pregnancy. Alison flipped, as her school friends would say!

How did he know, who told him, what gave him the right to...? Mr Stevenson was on the defensive and explained that Susan Moor had called to see her after speaking to her boyfriend, that it was in her best interests to talk about it, and so he went on. But Alison was already slamming the door to his office as she stormed out.

Susan Moor had always made a point of letting parents at Greencross School know that they were more than welcome to call around to see her if there were any problems they thought she could help with. She was not, however, expecting that evening's visit from Alison Smart and her parents. Susan was amazed as it transpired that the parents knew that Alison was pregnant, although they did not know who the father was. Alison had not wanted to tell them, and they had respected this.

They were now planning to move house some distance away where Alison could bring up her child in peace. If she wanted to later, she could get in touch with the father. After all, Alison had said enough for them to know she had misled him into thinking she was a lot older and that he was quite a caring person. They knew the law, but they would look after their daughter and, anyway, what good would come of getting the police involved?

Susan Moor could not really take in what she was hearing. She was faced with a family whose values were so removed from hers she couldn't believe it. What about the school and the standards? She soon came to, though, as Mrs. Smart made her point: 'You know, we were dealing with this reasonably well. We were all upset, but our plans were well laid and we would have got out of this without a problem — nobody needed to know. Now the school knows all about it; you should have kept your mouth shut. Call yourself a nurse — all you care about is your precious school, not our daughter; we could report you for this.'

## Outcome

Alison Smart and her parents left Susan Moor's home. She never saw or heard from them again, and they didn't report her. Susan isn't sure what happened to Alison and her baby to this day. She did go and see Mr Stevenson at the school, although contrary to his original concerns it would appear that he was only concerned about Alison while she was in his class. She had gone, and that was that.

Alan Salt never came back to the practice to see Susan either. Maybe Alison had got word to him and let him know the trouble she had so nearly caused. He was a distraught man and would benefit from counselling, although Susan was sure she would never see him again.

Susan Moor resigned from the Board of Governors, much to the suprise of her colleagues there, and she stopped doing her family planning clinic. The partners knew she had found this hard going on top of her other work, and they asked the other practice nurse to take it over, just as they had been trying to persuade Susan to let them do for some time.

Susan talked these events through with one of the professional advisers at the RCN, and eventually came to believe that she had been through a learning experience from which she should move forward. However it still stops her dead when a patient utters the words: 'nurse — I am so glad you could see me. I just wanted to talk to someone in confidence...'

## Discussion

Clause 10 of the UKCC *Code of Professional Conduct* (1992) emphasises that a nurse must:

> *'...protect all confidential information concerning patients and clients obtained in the course of professional practice and make disclosures only with consent, where required by the order of a court or where you can justify disclosure in the wider public interest;'*

No doubt Susan Moor did not remember these exact words as Alan Salt opened up his heart to her, but she did remember that she had to respect confidentiality. However, she was confused as to who was her patient or client. Alan was obviously in need of some support, although her mind concentrated on Alison Smart; she wasn't a patient of the practice but Susan had a responsibility to help her. The fact of the matter is that no matter whether the patient was Alan or Alison, Susan misjudged the need to override her responsibility to maintain confidentiality by involving Mr Stevenson, the teacher.

Susan Moor did admit later that her actions were more a result of her concern for Greencross School and what she was seeking to achieve through her work as a governor, i.e. high standards of education, discipline and morality, rather than her concern for either Alan Salt or Alison Smart, and it was this motivation that caused her to rush to the school and put her foot well and truly in it.

Of course, Alan had broken the law: he had had sex with a minor and admitted it freely, but it was not for Susan to judge him on this. She may have been able to persuade him to tell the police himself, but would this have helped matters? If Alan had admitted rape, things may have been different — remember the wider public interest clause in section 10 above. Alan never came back to the practice; would he have done anyway? Susan will never know what happened to him or what she could have done to help him.

Perhaps the attitude of Alison's parents was also something that Susan Moor could never have envisaged. Rather than seeing her as someone who was trying to help, they saw her as an interfering nuisance in a problem that the family had already begun to reconcile. Susan admitted to herself that they seemed to be caring parents and that they would look after their daughter, and that her letting the class teacher know about this could have made things worse for Alison. Susan Moor was surely a victim of that old adage of not being able to see the wood for the trees. She allowed her own value system, and concern for things that mattered to her, i.e. the school and its standards, colour her judgment.

The confidentiality clause of the *Code of Professional Conduct* is perhaps the most difficult to apply as there is so much potential for extenuating circumstances, especially when you consider the duties imposed by the rest of the *Code*. *Ethical Guidelines for Professional Practice* (UKCC 1996) sections 62–73 offers more guidance on how practitioners should approach such dilemmas and how and when to disclose confidential information.

If you find yourself in a similar situation to Susan Moor, take time to consider all the options and the possible consequences of all your actions carefully. Understand your own values and prejudices before you make a decision. Remember that things are not always what they seem, and for all your good intent you may well do more harm than good.

# Reference

UKCC (1996) *Ethical Guidelines for Clinical Practice*. UKCC, London

# Further reading

Bannon M, Carter Y (1991) Confidentiality and child protection. *Practitioner* **235**: 826, 828, 830–1

British Medical Association (GMSC), Health Education Authority, Family Planning Association, Royal College of General Practitioners (1994) Confidentiality and People Under 16. BMA(GMSC), HEA, FPA, RCGP, London

British Medical Journal (1988) GMC asked to reconsider advice on confidentiality and the under 16s, (General Medical Council's advice on under 16s contraception). *Br Med J* **292**: 778–9

Brykczynska G (1989) Informed consent, (The rights of a child and the implications for child/parent relationships). *Paediatric Nursing* **1**(5): 6–8

Dickson N (1994) Keep it confidential, (Teachers should be allowed to offer confidential contraceptive advice to under 16s). *Nursing Times* **90**(21): 28–9

Gillick V (1988) Confidentiality and young people. *Ethics and Medicine* **4**(2): 21–3

McConnell T (1994) Confidentiality and the law. *J Med Ethics* **20**(1): 47–9

Melia K (1988) To tell or not to tell, (The ethics of confidentiality). *Nursing Times and Nursing Mirror* **84**(30): 37–9

Morgan H (1988) Confidentiality and young people: a general practitioner's response. *Ethics and Medicine* **4**(2): 24–5

Scally G (1993) Confidentiality, contraception and young people. *Br Med J* **307**: 1157–8

Smith AM (1992) Consent to treatment in childhood. *Arch Dis Childhood* **67**(10): 1247–8; 419–24

Tingle J (1990) Nurses and the law: when to tell, (Confidentiality). *Nursing Times* **86**(35): 58–9

Torkington S (1989) Accountability and training in child protection work. *Senior Nurse* **9**(1): 10–11

UKCC Register (1987) Confidentiality, (And the code of nursing practice). *UKCC Register No 1 July*: 3–4

Wright S (1992) The case for confidentiality, (Legal aspects for nurses who whistleblow). *Nursing Standard* **6**(19): 52–3

# Case Study 6
# Practice Nurse Alicia Denton

## Key Issues and Concepts:

- Duty of Care
- Negligence

Practice Nurse Alicia Denton had a busy morning ahead of her. She was visiting the nearby residential home, for which the partners for whom she worked had responsibility. Generally, she quite enjoyed visiting the home, but today she wasn't looking forward to administering flu vaccines to a dozen or so residents, as she knew how hard it was to explain what they were for before going ahead and giving them.

Anyway, the job had to be done and Alicia loaded up the car and set off up the High Street. As she left the practice car park she noticed, out of the corner of her eye, a couple of children hurtling across the common on their mountain bikes and thought to herself that they were going far too fast and should be more careful. She drove a little further down the road and then it happened: the children had beaten her to the point where the path across the common meets the main road, but they hadn't beaten the car in front of her. With a peculiarly 'tinny' sound the car hit the bikes and their riders were sprawled out on the road.

It was all Alicia could do to put her brakes on hard and make an emergency stop, to the accompanying clatter of vials of flu vaccine, syringes and needles flying around the boot. She jumped out of the car to see what she could do. The driver of the vehicle which had hit the children had got out too, and was standing by the roadside wringing his hands; the children were still in the road, a little girl of about eight holding her knee and crying, and a boy of nine or so sitting on the pavement with his hands clasped over a nasty graze on his leg, trying desperately not to cry.

Alicia quickly ascertained that both children were not seriously hurt, and another passer-by was already summoning an ambulance. Alicia comforted the little girl, who by now was just sobbing occasionally, and proceeded to get her first-aid bag out of the car to tend to the boy's leg wound. She took out a container of antiseptic wipes and began to clean the graze; the boy's resilience faltered and macho pretence disintegrated into tears — somewhat louder than his younger friend — as the wound began to sting.

Alicia finished cleaning the wound and thought to herself how late she now was for her visit to the home. She explained to the woman who had called the ambulance that she would have to go and asked her to stay with the children until it arrived. She put her first-aid kit back in the car and went off to do the vaccinations.

Doing the vaccinations was as bad as she thought it would be; it took ages to explain the purpose of the injections to the residents, and she hated putting a needle into some of them as they were so thin. But it was a job well done, and she packed up, said goodbye to all and returned to the surgery for her lunch. 'What a morning — and the afternoon yet to come!' she thought to herself . Little did she know what the afternoon would bring.

Shortly after lunch, a worried-sounding receptionist rang through to Alicia's room to say that two CID officers were in the waiting room and wished to 'interview' her about a most serious matter. Alicia smiled to herself as she knew that they would want to talk about the accident she had helped out with, and told the receptionist to send them through. She welcomed the two men at her door. They didn't look too happy to be seeing her, she thought.

The officers introduced themselves as DCs Sollitt and Andrews. DC Sollitt refused her offer to take a seat and began to explain why they were there. 'I'll get straight to the point,' he said. 'We have had a serious allegation that you assaulted a young boy this morning shortly after he had been injured in a road traffic accident.' 'What on earth is he going on about?' thought Alicia as she slumped into her chair. DC Andrews remained motionless in his seat, with an expression as hard as stone, while his colleague continued with his statement. It transpired that the young boy who was injured was the son of a local pharmacist, Mr Mansoor. He had arrived on the scene of the accident shortly after Alicia had left, just as the ambulance arrived. He accompanied his son to hospital where it was discovered that he had a lump of gravel embedded in his leg.

The doctor at the hospital asked the boy about his injury, and whether it hurt or not. He had replied that he didn't feel much 'until the nurse rubbed it and made it sting'. The doctor commented that the gravel was actually under the skin and looked as if it had been pushed in. To cut a long story short, the pharmacist believed that Alicia had made his son's injury worse as a result of her first-aid actions, and he now wanted to press a charge of assault. At this point the stony-faced DC Andrews piped up that they were obliged to investigate, and that they had managed to trace her as another onlooker to the accident had recognised her in her uniform and knew which practice she was from — and why did she leave in such a hurry anyway?

Alicia was totally taken aback and tried to explain the situation. She chanced upon the accident, she did what she thought was the right thing, the boy had felt a stinging sensation as she had used a chlorhexidine-impregnated wipe, and she really hadn't seen any gravel in his wound — but then again she was in a rush.

## Outcome

The two detectives listened carefully as Alicia explained what she had done. Eventually they recognised that she had acted in good faith, but Mr Mansoor had made a complaint following the casualty doctor's comment that the gravel looked as if it had been pushed in. The detectives realised that Alicia had done her best and it was just a matter of convincing Mr Mansoor. Alicia suggested that she met him personally to explain, although the officers didn't think this would be a good idea. However, Alicia insisted and they drove round to Mr Mansoor's home.

Mr Mansoor was very angry to begin with and shouted at Alicia; however DC Andrews stepped in and explained Alicia's side of the story. Mrs Mansoor also remonstrated with her husband, and eventually he began to calm down. The atmosphere really changed when the Mansoor's son came into the room and said 'thank you for helping me, nurse'. Mr Mansoor looked bemused at this; the police officers looked at each other and shrugged their shoulders.

After a good deal of confusion, and some tears — even on the part of Mr Mansoor, everyone in the room began to realise that the situation had got totally out of hand. Mr Mansoor saw that the anger he felt for the car driver and his distress at the thought of what could have happened to his son was misdirected at Alicia. Alicia realised that maybe she should have taken a little more time and care when attending to the Mansoor's son's leg wound, although she felt that she did the best she could in the circumstances. The CID officers realised that they were not needed; however, they did advise Alicia that she should have waited until the ambulance arrived, or at least given her name and contact details to someone. After all, she was a crucial witness to the accident.

A little while later, Alicia sat in her office as she thought about her work for the following day. She wondered to herself whether it was actually worth the effort of going out of one's way to help others — and decided that it was.

## Discussion

Again we have an example of a practice nurse who was the victim of bizarre circumstances. This could have happened to any nurse but it just happened to be Alicia Denton, practice nurse, who was passing by. Was it worth her stopping to help, and what could she have done to avoid the situation in which she later found herself?

Contrary to popular belief, there is no duty placed upon a nurse, or anyone else for that matter, to stop and assist at the scene of an accident. The so-called 'duty of care' only exists if there is a pre-existing relationship between those involved, e.g. if the nurse had caused the accident or had been specifically employed to render assistance in such circumstances. There is no law which said that Alicia had to stop and help; however, she did so out of a sense of moral/ethical duty.

Alicia did have to bear in mind her UKCC *Code of Professional Conduct*; remember this places an **'at all times'** responsibility on the nurse to act in the best interests of patients and clients and serve the interests of society. The UKCC indicate that while, as a nurse, you do not have a legal responsibility to offer assistance in such instances, 'you must answer professionally for what you do or do not do', and that 'you must use your common sense and professional judgement to decide how involved you get and whether you are able to help' (UKCC, 1996).

Even though Alicia was not obliged to stop, as she had no duty of care, in the eyes of the law as soon as she had intervened to assist the Mansoor's son she had assumed that duty. Similarly, we could argue that the boy now became her patient. So did Alicia act properly, or was the angry Mr Mansoor right to involve the police?

As soon as Alicia became involved, she was expected to help the boy to the standard that we would expect from any reasonable person. As such, Alicia used her first-aid kit to the best of her abilities, as would any other passing motorist; she rushed and missed a piece of gravel, but would any other ordinary person have done any better? However, had Alicia arrived at the scene of the accident and professed her knowledge as a competent first-aider, pushing her way through the crowd to assist, then things may well have been different as she would have put herself above the standard expected of any reasonable person.

We can be pretty certain that none of this crossed Mr Mansoor's mind when he called the police. He was simply looking for some means of venting his anger, although his accusation of assault could have been technically proven (with some difficulty) if it could not have been shown that Alicia was acting in the best interests of his son. If Alicia had been employed to work in an emergency response situation and had attended the accident in that capacity, then maybe Mr Mansoor could have pressed a case of professional negligence with more success.

If Mr Mansoor was seeking to exploit the finer points of the 'duty of care' principle, then the CID officers certainly were not; they were simply responding to his complaint. Once the situation had become clear, they were not interested in taking any action against Alicia, although their advice to her that she should have waited for the ambulance to arrive or leave her details was sensible enough.

To conclude then, Alicia did her best and that was good enough. In a way the fact that she was a nurse was immaterial; however, it is in such first-aid situations that nurses occasionally find themselves in difficulty as the general public believe they should be competent to assist, even though it is rare for a nurse to receive first-aid training during her student days.

If you find yourself in a similar situation to Alicia, take care not to overstep the mark: do what you can in a competent manner but do not try to be a superhero, unless of course you have the knowledge required to be one. A grazed leg may not be serious nor present too many problems (unless you are as unfortunate as Alicia), but think twice before you whip out the penknife and have a go at emergency surgery at the roadside. Remember: do what would be expected of an ordinary reasonable person not prime contender for 'first-aider of the year' award.

# References

UKCC (1996) *Ethical Guidelines for Professional Practice*. UKCC, London

# Further reading

Barber J (1993) Legal aspects of first aid and emergency care: 1, (Nurses' duty to administer first aid outside the professional environment). *Br J Nursing* **2**(12): 641–2

Dimond B (1993) Legal aspects of first aid and emergency care: 2, (Nurse's legal duty to offer first aid). *Br J Nursing* **2**(13): 692–4

Tingle J (1991) First aid law, (Legal position of an off-duty nurse who administers first aid to an accident victim). *Nursing Times* **87**(35): 48–9

# Case study 7
# Practice Nurse Victoria Swan

## Key Issues and Concepts:

- Unfitness to practice due to illness

There was a lull in the previously steady stream of patients coming into the surgery that morning which gave Ethel and Andrea, the two receptionists on duty, the opportunity to catch up on their usual observations of life in the practice.

Ethel noted that Sister Edmunds (the district nurse team leader) appeared rather more harassed than usual, and nothing like her normal, organised self. 'You know what that is,' commented Andrea. 'They've all been given these new-fangled computer things to log up their work . Have you not seen them? 'They are a bit like our Simon's Game Boy.' The district nurses had indeed all been issued with hand-held computers into which they had to input their daily activities. Sister Edmunds was finding this particularly difficult; she claimed it had taken the best part of five years for her to master her video recorder at home.

'But what about Sister Swan?' interjected Ethel, rapidly changing the subject as she was not a great new technology buff herself and sensed that her colleague was about to launch into some diatribe about Simon's computer games and how he could programme their video at four years old, etc. 'Doesn't she seem a lot perkier today,' Ethel continued. Andrea thought for a minute and replied: 'You know something — she really does. Maybe whatever it was that's been bothering her has cleared up... she never mentioned anything about it you know...' The conversation between the two receptionists continued on and off as they discussed the miracle recovery of their practice nurse, and just about everything else, in between marshalling patients to the various doors in the surgery.

Victoria Swan had a rather boring white door to her room, not that she was particularly bothered. In fact, she was rather pleased to have her own consulting room having heard from colleagues in other practices who seem to work from cupboards under the stairs. Victoria chuckled to herself. She did feel happy today, and looking in her reflection she had to agree with Ethel and Andrea that she looked a hundred times better today (they had broken the good news to her as she emerged for the notes of patients booked to see her).

A hundred times better than she looked on Friday is what they had meant. Friday had been the culmination of a week of disasters. On Monday she had been greeted by a letter from her ex-husband's solicitor seeking to enhance the access arrangements to their daughter. Tuesday had seen the childminder carted off to hospital, having fallen off a step-ladder, and on Wednesday she had heard from the University that she had flunked two module essays she had submitted at the end of year one of her Masters. Ethel and Andrea had always been at pains to point out that she had bitten off more than she could chew, but she knew, or at least thought she knew, that she could handle it. Anyway, even though Thursday had brought no catastrophies, her world was in such a mess that by Friday she had looked and felt 90 and had pleaded with the senior partner to let her go home early.

Well, that was last week. 'What time is it now?' Victoria asked herself looking at the wall clock. 'Good, time to take another dose.' Victoria took the bottle from her pocket and popped another of the bright blue pills into her mouth. 'Thank God for Alex,' she thought out loud.

Alex had been a friend of her ex-husband. He was a kind of artist-cum-sculptor, and since her divorce he had conveniently transferred his friendship to her. She knew that he wanted to be more than good friends, but he hadn't said anything so far. On Friday night, though, she had called him out of desperation, and he had managed to get the pills from a friend of his who had had similar problems to her. He had said that she would have to pay for them, but that could wait until she got paid.

The pills made Victoria feel great: all the problems of the last week had disappeared, in fact all the problems in the practice had gone away and she felt so much happier about everything. Victoria brought her bottle of blue pills to the practice every day, and looked up at the clock on her wall with ever-increasing frequency to determine when she could take the next one. It wasn't long before she had to get another bottle from Alex, and then another, as she needed to keep one at the surgery because she had started to forget to bring the one from home. Forgetfulness was really getting to be a problem. One afternoon she had found herself engineering a bizarre conversation with Ethel about the sort of problems the patients had come in with that morning in the hope that she would mention their names and remind her who she had seen.

Some four weeks on from Victoria Swan's disaster week, Ethel and Andrea did not need to employ their finely tuned powers of observation, as their practice nurse all but stumbled through the surgery door and into her room, with something approaching a grunt in their direction as she passed.

Alex's source of supply of the blue pills had finally called in the debt, and not being one to mess with his sort, Alex had not wasted time in making Victoria aware of this. As a result, she had been working Friday through to Sunday nights as an agency nurse in an attempt to generate the not inconsiderable amount of money she now required to pay back her 'friend'.

Ethel and Andrea, after some deliberation, decided that it would be for Victoria's own good if they were to tell Dr Meadows, the senior partner, what a state they had seen her in. Dr Meadows raised an eyebrow as Ethel emphasised that 'while they were not ones to pry' they felt that the practice nurse was really ill and that he should have a word with her about her condition.

Dr Meadows agreed that he would do so, although while they had been talking Victoria had ushered a patient into her room. The patient left the nurse's room, leaving the door ajar, and Dr Meadows walked in. He hadn't seen Victoria for a few days as he had been away on a course, but he could barely recognise the woman he had worked with for the last eight years. As he opened the door, Victoria was putting two bright blue pills into her mouth, her eyes firmly fixed on the clock on the wall. She saw Dr. Meadows out of the corner of her eye, but continued to take the pills, and pour out some water to swallow them with, spilling most of it in the process as she fought to control her shaking hand.

'Victoria...what the...?' Dr Meadows was stopped in his tracks as Victoria slumped into his arms.

## Outcome

A week later Dr Meadows visited his practice nurse in hospital (reluctantly carrying a toy rabbit and get well card from Ethel and Andrea. She still looked pretty rough, she was still shaking, but not as badly as before, and her drip had just been taken down. Victoria wanted to tell him about everything, even though he insisted that she need not. She explained the problems she had been facing, and even though she knew he had been so supportive in the past — fixing her hours to suit her childminder, letting her go on the course, and everything — she hadn't been able to find it in her to tell him. She told of Alex and the pills. She had always suspected that they were amphetamines but kept telling herself that she would just use them to tide her over. She was so sorry that she had gone to work like she was — think of what she could have done to the patients. She was resigning and she never wanted to nurse again. Dr Meadows reassured her and told her not to worry about all that just now. 'Let's get you better first,' he stressed.

Strange as it may seem, Victoria actually did a pretty good job at the practice until the morning she collapsed, considering her growing addiction to the blue pills. However, when she eventually did get better she did not return to her job, or to nursing at all. Dr. Meadows was sure in his mind that even though Victoria had been very ill she had still been competent in her work; however, as she had resigned, what more could he do?

## Discussion

Nursing is a stressful occupation at the best of times, and practice nursing can be particularly hectic, even without the compounding factor of a week of disaster such as that experienced by Victoria Swan. She should certainly have talked to someone about her problems before she got as far as taking her friend Alex's way out, i.e. the blue pills. However, Victoria knew that some secrets were hard to keep at the practice. The receptionists were renowned for gossiping, and even though Dr. Meadows had warned them about it, she was still reluctant to share her feelings with anyone. It was unfortunate that Victoria did not ask for advice until she was recuperating from her illness and considering her future in nursing.

Victoria knew in her heart that she didn't want to go back to nursing, and she questioned whether she would have ever been well enough to do so or have the confidence to see patients again. She knew that she had come very close to causing one of her patients real harm and being found to be in breach of her *Code of Professional Conduct*.

No complaint was made about Victoria Swan, and she hadn't harmed a patient. She also left the nursing profession of her own accord, but what could she have done to avoid this situation?

We have suggested that she could have spoken to one of the partners at her practice, and explained why she didn't. Victoria could have contacted her membership organisation — The RCN — for advice, either from one of its community health advisers, or from its confidential counselling service, Nurseline. This could have provided an outlet other than the drugs to which she resorted. She could also have contacted the nurse adviser/facilitator at the FHSA. Another option, which may sound rather strange, would have been to 'report' herself to the UKCC. This would be a rare occurrence, but not necessarily a bad option.

No matter how Victoria had come to the attention of the UKCC, its duty would be to investigate the case. Under the terms of section 12 of the Nurses, Midwives and Health Visitors Act 1979, the UKCC is required to make rules governing the circumstances and the means by which a person's name may be removed from the register. In response to this requirement, the UKCC provides two means of dealing with nurses deemed to have transgressed the code of conduct. On the one hand, an individual who is alleged to have committed an act of misconduct could find his/her case being referred to a Professional Conduct Committee for a public hearing, and on the other an individual who is considered unfit to practice due to illness could find his/her case being referred to a health committee (see Chapter 4).

In Victoria Swan's case, if she had harmed a patient or been reported to the UKCC by any individual suspecting her to be unfit to practise due to illness, whether this was her original stress condition or the drug addiction it led to, or if she had chosen to report herself, it is almost certain that her case would have proceeded along the Health Committee route.

In summary, the Health Committee would arrange for medical examinations to be undertaken by members of a panel of medical examiners maintained by the UKCC for this purpose. Once the case is before the Committee the hearing is conducted in private and the individual is presented with the findings of the examiners. Each case before the Health Committee is the subject of detailed consideration and any illness that results in serious impairment of fitness to practise can result in removal from the register.

However, in Victoria's case she may well have been able to demonstrate that she had had insight into her problems and had come forward before she caused any harm, and the UKCC had assisted her in receiving the care she required. However, her ability to continue to practise would still be questioned.

The simple message behind the example of Victoria Swan is to ask for help without shame or embarrassment as soon as you even start to think you have a problem. There are sources of confidential advice you can go to without having to rely on a way out such as that offered to Victoria by Alex and his blue pills. You may think this could never happen to you but the RCN does receive calls from nurses, who, while not quite so bad as Victoria, have found themselves in situations where they feel the light at the end of the tunnel is very dim indeed. Unlike this case, it is often the feelings of temptation towards drugs that are available within the practice that sparks these calls. Practice nurses do not make that many calls of this sort, thank goodness, but we would rather nurses call with a small problem as soon as they are aware of it, than for us to try and help when things have reached Victoria Swan proportions.

# Further reading

Faugier J (1992) The hidden illness, (Problems and policies of alcohol and drug abuse in health
    service staff). *Nursing Times* **88**(19): 24

Heath J (1993) High risks, (Alcohol or drug abuse in the workplace). *Occupational Safety and
    Health* **23**(3): 13–7

Lucas G (1989) Substance abuse in the workplace. *Occupational Health* **41**(12): 355–6

Occupational Health Bulletin (1990) HSE guidance booklet 'Drug Abuse at Work'. *Occupational
    Health Review* **27**: 9–12

# Case Study 8
# Practice Nurse Carol Teale

## Key Issues and Concepts:

- Duty of care
- Negligence
- Employment rights

Carol breathed a sigh of relief as she drove into the surgery car park — for once there was a free space. It did irritate her a little to see the row of 'Doctor Parking Only' bays standing empty on most days when she had to jostle with patients for a space. She had already had four parking tickets this year when she had been forced to park on the road, and even writing in on headed paper had had no effect on the fines she received. Today, though, as Carol glanced back at her brand-new car which the partners had just bought for her, she felt that she could forgive them for hogging all the decent spaces.

It had taken Carol at least six months to negotiate the purchase, convincing the partners that she was doing more and more work outside the surgery, and that they really should provide her with a car. She had had to make all the arrangements herself: ordering the vehicle, registering it in her name, etc. All Dr Simpson had had to do was write out the cheque but she could still see the pain and anguish on his face.

Anyway, the car was making a great difference to her work, particularly as the high ratio of elderly people and the three retirement homes in the practice population meant that she spent a lot of time visiting for over-75 checks and to provide immunisations and do some dressings. This afternoon she had another series of assessments to do, the first being to a dear old lady, Martha Fox, who lived up a potholed lane behind the farm just outside the village.

Carol cursed under her breath as her new car bounced and scraped its way to Mrs Fox's home at the top of the hill. As ever, Martha was in a jovial mood. In addition to her routine assessment, Carol was due to give her patient a vitamin injection which had been prescribed by one of the doctors. However, Mrs Fox apologised profusely as her son had not yet taken the scrip down to the chemist, and so there was no injection to give. But Martha had thought of a way around the problem. 'You know, nurse,' she said, 'I would quite enjoy a little trip out in the new car you have been telling me about. We could just pop down to the chemist in the village and get my jab.' It was a nice sunny day, and Carol knew Martha didn't get out much. She knew that if she didn't give her the jab now she would only have to come back tomorrow, and the chemist was only at the bottom of the hill.

Carol helped Mrs Fox into the front seat of her car and they set off down the lane. It seemed even bumpier going down, and Carol was aware that having Mrs Fox in the front was causing the car to lean to one side (as Martha was always reminding her, she was a 'well-built' woman). Carol had just returned her eyes to the road, having made an instant guess at Mrs Fox's body mass index through the rear view mirror, when a tractor turned out in front of her. She swore very loudly and hit the brakes. The car slid along the road and down the hill, eventually coming to rest when a front tyre hit a large stone at the side of the road. Carol was out of the car in a flash. 'Thank God for that,' she exclaimed; she had stopped a yard from the tractor and the car was not damaged at all. 'You want to take more care in that little shiny motor of yours,' the farmer advised 'It wouldn't look all that good if you'd gone into my tractor here now, would it!'

Carol ignored this helpful advice and got back in the car as the farmer backed the tractor out of the way. Mrs Fox was cradling her elbow and looked to be in pain. 'What's wrong Martha?' Carol enquired. 'Oh nothing dear,' Mrs Fox reassured her. 'Its just that when you stopped so quick I banged my arm on the front of the car here.' She pointed to the dashboard, which was actually quite well padded, and Carol was eventually convinced that Martha was all right. They carried on with their trip and Mrs Fox was eventually given her vitamin injection.

## Outcome

Martha Fox's elbow continued to ache a little into that evening, although it really was nothing serious. However, when her son called in to see her to collect the prescription he had forgotten the day before, he was none too pleased as his mother told the story of the nurse in her nice new car sliding down their lane and just missing Alec Simpson in his tractor. He resolved to make a complaint to the practice.

Mrs Fox's son saw Dr Simpson, the senior partner in the practice, the next day and alleged that Carol Teale had caused his mother to be injured through her poor driving. Dr Simpson undertook to investigate the incident and offered to pay Mrs Fox a visit to check on her arm. The son said that this was the least he could do and that Dr Simpson would be hearing from his solicitors.

The solicitor's letter arrived some days later. It was a standard format and basically sought compensation from the practice for the pain and discomfort caused to Martha Fox as she was injured in Carol's car. Dr Simpson huffed when he saw that one of his friends and colleagues had submitted a report on the injury to the solicitor. The letter suggested that this was a minor matter and the solicitor was sure that it could be dealt with through the practice's motor insurance policy.

Dr Simpson discussed this matter with a very flustered Carol Teale. He reassured her, reiterating the solicitor's view that this was merely an insurance matter. There was a problem for Carol, however. As part of the deal with the partners for her to get a new car, she had agreed to undertake all the arrangements, and the car would be registered in her name and notionally belong to her, not the practice, with the partners simply paying for it. One thing that Carol had not done was to discuss her insurance requirements properly with her broker.

Carol had objected to using her own car for practice business, and had never done so. When she got the new car she simply passed on the details of the vehicle to the insurers and paid an additional premium. As such, her comprehensive insurance for her social and domestic use only had been transferred to the new car. Carol was not covered for any third party liability when her vehicle was being used for business purposes.

The insurance company refused to meet the claim from Mrs Fox's solicitor, and eventually Carol had to make a payment of £900.00 out of her own pocket as the partners contended that she should have taken out appropriate insurance, and that she should not have been carrying patients in her car anyway.

## Discussion

Unfortunately for Carol Teale, the partners had a point. It was not a requirement of her job to ferry around passengers, whether the car was provided by the practice or not. She had been keen to let Mrs Fox have a ride in her new car, and taking her to the chemist to collect the prescription did save her time in the long run.

Even if it had been practice policy that Carol should take passengers, she should have made sure that her car insurance was adequate to cover third party liability for business use. She would have had a good case to ask the practice to pay for this. Carol was compromised as the practice had merely provided the money to buy the car so they could not be held responsible for not taking out the insurance.

If Mrs Fox had been seriously injured, Carol could have been paying out a lot more than £900, and if she had hit a pedestrian she could have found herself meeting major damages claims and perhaps defending a driving charge without the back-up of an insurance company, as well as having to pay all the legal fees.

It is important to check exactly what your insurance covers you for when using either your own vehicle for work purposes, or one provided by the practice for your use. Often the difference in premiums is quite small, but unless the insurer is aware that you use the vehicle for business use they can be very reluctant to assist in a case such as Carol Teale's.

If the practice requires you to use your own vehicle, ask your employer to pay the extra insurance cost. The employer should also pay for petrol used on practice business, and it would not be unreasonable for you to claim payment towards the road fund licence (tax disc) and depreciation of the vehicle caused by usage above and beyond that which would occur if you only drove it for your own domestic use.

If the practice intends to provide a vehicle, it is far better for it to be purchased or leased in the name of the practice, and for the insurance to be arranged on your behalf by the practice. This is usually a better option than that taken by Carol Teale's employers (simply giving her the money) as the practice should be able to offset the purchase/lease and running costs against tax. If you are allowed to use the car outside of work then you will have to come to some arrangement with the practice about petrol costs, and your contribution to wear and tear etc. You may also be taxed on the 'benefit' of being provided with a 'company car' — check with your tax office or financial adviser.

Do check these small but potentially serious points. Carol Teale may well have got away with Mrs Fox having only a bruised elbow if it hadn't been for her stroppy son, but what if she had killed someone on the way to a visit the next day?

# Further reading

Curnoyer CP (1985) Protecting yourself legally after a patient's injured, (Writing an incident report). *Nursing Life* **5**(2): 18–22

# Case Study 9
# Practice Nurse Irene Neil

## Key Issues and Concepts:

- Ensuring safety of patients
- Environment of care
- Health and safety at work

Practice nurse Irene Neil was enjoying her afternoon off from the surgery and had decided to spend some time in her garden. 'Ouch!' she cried out as one of the roses she was pruning fought back and gouged a nasty scratch in her thumb. At that, Irene decided to call it a day.

Having patched herself up, Irene made a cup of tea and decided to catch up with some TV programmes she had videotaped over the past few days. At the end of her viewing, she put down her empty cup and contemplated the programme she had just finished watching. It was part of the RCN 'Nursing Update' series and mostly concerned wound care. She was intrigued that all the nurses in the programme wore gloves when dealing with their patients, and in fact the narrator had commented that it was essential for nurses to do so when there was even the slightest risk of coming into contact with body fluids. She never wore gloves at work for dressing wounds, and certainly not for taking blood samples — it would be so cumbersome.

What did worry Irene, however, was the point made in the programme that it was especially important for nurses with any cuts or grazes on their hands to take precautions, for their own sake and that of their patients. Irene looked down at the cut inflicted by the rose, stretching a good three inches along the side of her thumb. She made a mental note that she would have to find some gloves in the surgery tomorrow before starting her clinic.

Next morning Irene found a box of polythene gloves under the sink in the treatment room. They were a bit flimsy and hard to get on straight, but they would do. But by coffee time, and half a dozen patients later, Irene was fed up messing around with the gloves — they were next to useless. She had torn four pairs trying to get them on, and even when intact they filled up with moisture. Irene really couldn't do her work as well while wearing them. However, the TV programme echoed in her ears, and she decided that she would have to ask the practice manager to get one of the staff to go to the chemist and buy a box of the latex rubber-type in her own size; at least then she would be able to protect herself and maintain some degree of dexterity.

Like most things in their practice, her request was not seen as being at all straightforward by the practice manager. 'We've never used gloves in the treatment room before,' she said. Irene replied somewhat sarcastically: 'No, I know you haven't, but I feel that I need to use them, particularly as I have this cut.' She showed the manager the damage the thorn had done. 'Nasty!' came the reply. 'We will have to see what Dr James says about this'. Irene sighed with despair; she really didn't know why the practice wasted its money on a manager — she wouldn't sneeze without asking one of the partners first, let alone make a decision as 'significant' as buying a box of gloves.

## Outcome

To Irene's suprise, a few minutes later the practice manager emerged triumphant from Dr James' office. Apparently he had agreed with her that there was no clinical need for Irene to wear gloves, and that the standard of her technique should ensure that there is no infection risk to or from a patient. Irene was having none of it and went to see the doctor herself.

Unfortunately, Dr James was not exactly helpful. 'What do you need gloves for anyway?' he enquired. 'It's not as if we have any AIDS patients or anything is it now?' Irene really could not believe her ears and set about explaining the principles of infection to the GP, and in particular that it was impossible to predict which patients had AIDS as they walked into the surgery, even though this was not the issue as far as she was concerned. She simply wanted to wear the gloves as a matter of good practice, and to cover her injury. Dr James persisted with the AIDS line of defence for not allowing the purchase of gloves. 'Look here, if you have a thing about touching infectious patients you shouldn't be in nursing anyway. You can't refuse to touch people just because they have AIDS you know. Anyway, when did you last see me wearing gloves with my patients — horrible things!' (Irene assumed he meant the gloves, although she could not be sure.)

Irene felt as if she was just about to let rip at this intransigence and totally irrational argument, when Dr James stopped her dead in her tracks: 'If you really feel that you can't be a proper nurse without wearing rubber gloves, then I think we had better think about finding someone more suitable' was his final contribution to the discussion. Irene knew she was getting nowhere and this implicit threat over what she thought was such a small detail was just too much. She slammed the door and left the doctor peering into his magazine, just as he was when she first went in. As it was the RCN programme that had sparked all this off, Irene felt that she should contact the organisation for further advice before trying to take on Dr James again.

Irene's interpretation of the RCN Nursing Update programme was accurate. The College advises that all nurses performing activities through which they may come into contact with body fluids of patients should wear gloves, and that care should be taken to cover cuts and grazes, no matter how superficial. The flimsy polythene type of glove is not ideal because of the problems Irene Neil experienced. Latex rubber gloves are the best solution; these should be sterile if undertaking a procedure where aseptic technique is crucial, or simply hygienically clean for doing other types of work.

The outcome of Irene Neil's case was pretty straightforward. Armed with the above information she confronted her employer and made a well reasoned request for the gloves yet again. Dr. James remained impassive but agreed to check this out with the GP adviser at the FHSA who said she would be delighted to visit the practice to discuss this further.

The GP adviser came the following day, and although Dr James didn't allow Irene into the meeting, it soon became obvious to her that he had been 'enlightened' by his colleague. That afternoon the practice manager somewhat coyly drew Irene's attention to the copy of the FHSA infection control guidelines the adviser had left behind, and let her know that a supply of gloves would be ordered.

## Discussion

It might seem rather extreme that a gardening injury, with a rose thorn pricking not just Irene Neil's thumb but also her conscience, could lead to such a confrontation within the practice team. However, this is another case dealt with by the RCN recently. Like most problems faced by nurses in general practice, a good deal of aggravation could have been avoided by the parties concerned, i.e. GP, nurse and practice manager, having a rational discussion. On so many occasions, however, this doesn't happen because of either lack of time or some personality conflict.

Irene's supposedly simple request was legitimately grounded in the Health and Safety at Work Act 1974 (HSAW) and her UKCC *Code of Professional Conduct*. Under her code of conduct, Irene has a duty to 'act always in such a manner as to promote and safeguard the interests and well-being of patients and clients' (clause 1) and, ensure that 'no act or omission on your part, or within your sphere of responsibility, is detrimental to the interests, condition or safety of patients and clients' (clause 2). Clearly Irene's desire to cover her hand wound when dealing with patients could be seen to be motivated by these requirements, and so her request for suitable gloves was quite reasonable.

On the other side of the coin, the HSAW places a duty on Irene Neil's employer, Dr James, to take care of the health and safety of his employees. Under common law duty he is required to make sure that the practice premises and any equipment are safe, and that safe systems of work are implemented. In seeking to fulfil this duty Dr James must ensure that all reasonable practical precautions are taken to safeguard the employee, in this case the practice nurse. This includes the provision of protective clothing reasonably necessary to ensure the safety of the employee, i.e. latex gloves for Irene Neil.

Dr James could try to persist in his argument that Irene adopt a non-touch technique; however, this does not seem at all reasonable and Irene's request for gloves can be substantiated by examples of good practice in other clinical areas. Irene would have little trouble in showing that the polythene gloves were not adequate to protect her (let alone her patients) and that the latex alternatives would be more effective at a reasonable cost. If the doctor had carried out his threat to sack Irene as a result of her insistence on wearing gloves, it could be argued that his actions as an employer were unreasonable and that this was unfair dismissal. Irene could take her case to an industrial tribunal.

Dr James' comment regarding AIDS was most irregular. To accuse Irene of wanting to wear gloves because she was afraid of contracting HIV virus was ridiculous. Of course she should be aware of this and take all necessary precautions. But for Dr James to confidently assert that the practice had no such patients was a clear indication of his lack of awareness about infection control, in particular that the body fluids of all patients should be treated with care, not just because of HIV, but because of other risks such as hepatitis B, for example. As a matter of note, if Irene had refused to care for AIDS patients, as Dr James implied, then her professionalism could be called into question.

Irene did the right thing in not 'letting rip' at the GP; she collected the evidence she needed to make a cogent case, and when faced with her logical rationale, Dr James had little option but to consent to the provision of gloves. Irene's code of conduct insisted she do something, the Health and Safety at Work Act was on her side, and Dr James could well have found himself in breach of it. Maybe Dr James should have also looked to his own code of conduct before lecturing his practice nurse about her's.

## Further reading

British Medical Association (1988) *Rights and Responsibilities of Doctors*, (Sec.4.5. Responsibilities Imposed by the Health and Safety at Work etc. Act 1974). British Medical Association, London

Cooke RA, Hodgson ES (1992) General practitioners and health and safety at work, (Some doctors are unaware or choose to ignore their legal responsibilities under the Health and Safety at Work Act). *Br Med J* **305**: 1044

East J (1992) Implementing the COSHH regulations, (Nurses' responsibilities under COSHH (Control Of Substances Hazardous to Health) regulations, with special reference to infection control). *Nursing Standard* **6**(26): 33–5

# Case Study 10
# Practice Nurse Carol Moor

## Key Issues and Concepts

- Environment of Care
- Health and Safety at Work

Carol Moor worked in a single-handed practice in a remote rural area of The Midlands. She got on well with her GP employer, Dr Davison, who was well respected by his patients. The practice was curiously furnished with items of antique porcelain; Dr Davison was well known for having an eye for a bargain and his collection represented numerous visits to local sales. To her knowledge, Carol only knew of one unsavoury incident in the practice when one of the younger patients managed to decapitate one of the finer pieces and the GP's remonstrations with the mother were brushed aside with her curse, 'if you weren't so daft to have them in here it would never have happened would it?'

Carol Moor often felt that Dr Davison's eye for a bargain extended to her. She had been working flat out all week running her surgery and various clinics, and now she was going to spend all day catching up on the smears. She had been trying to convince the doctor for ages that he should get someone to help her parttime, but his only response was that he would help out if needs be. Unfortunately the patients didn't see it quite like this and always asked to see her.

To make matters worse, Carol knew that she was going to be frustrated by the fact that the practice only had three specula, which were of different sizes. The silly thing was that the treatment room was equipped with a bigger than average autoclave. Even though Dr Davison had bought this at a bargain price from a colleague in the next village who had retired, it had still cost hundreds of pounds and Carol was irritated that he could not see the sense in spending out on more instruments to put in it.

At the end of the session, Carol Moor sat back on her stool and sighed. It had been just as she had predicted; all the women she had called in had turned up and she had them waiting down the hall while the three specula went through the sterilisation cycle time. The autoclave reminded her of the washing machine at home which always seemed to take ten times as long to let her in when she was in a hurry. This machine seemed to wait ages after it had finished sterilising as it had an automatic cooling mechanism which protracted the cycle. This was a real waste of her time, and even though patients benefited from having the time to chat with her, many were waiting far too long. She really had to do something about this.

A telephone call to a selection of companies brought a rainforest of brochures from medical equipment companies tumbling through the practice letter box within a couple of days. Carol had made a specific effort to intercept these before Dr Davison, and she was now in a position to present him with a detailed list of specula available and their costs, particularly the 'bargain' prices for multiple purchases which she thought would appeal. However, the response was the usual 'I'll have to think about it Carol'. Carol valiantly tried to explain how much time she and her patients were wasting as they waited for the autoclave to finish its cycle, but to no avail.

Carol continued her three-specula sessions for a few weeks, doing the best she could under the circumstances. However, three of the women she had taken smears from came back to the surgery complaining of vaginal discharge which, following investigation, turned out to be candidal infection.

Carol knew that she had been diligent in her work, particularly as she knew what a pain it was to have to wait for the autoclave to produce the instruments for her use. 'But wait a minute...,' she thought to herself. Suddenly she had a flash of inspiration. She had cursed under her breath that morning at having to drag the hot instruments from the autoclave and do her best to cool them down for immediate use. But that hadn't been such a problem in the past, she thought. Why not?

Of course, the instruments should not have come out of the autoclave until they had gone through that long and boring cooling cycle. Carol let Dr Davison know that she thought there was a problem with the autoclave and asked whether he had a guarantee with it when he bought it from the other practice. Dr Davison mumbled a response about the GP he bought it from being an old friend and that he didn't think he needed a guarantee, so Carol asked what service arrangements he had made. Dr Davison replied that these new machines were reliable and that service contracts were a waste of money. Carol pointed out that their machine was now unreliable and that she would have to call the engineer. Dr Davison said nothing.

As arranged, the autoclave service engineer called the next day, and Carol explained the problem. The engineer used a test package with marker strips to test the machine. At the end of the cycle the engineer removed the package and showed no suprise as he announced that the machine had not sterilised it. It was obvious to him that the cycle had not been long enough. 'It's a wonder you haven't burnt yourself with this', he said. 'This new model is meant to cool them down before you can get your hands on them,' the engineer retorted. Just like my washing, thought Carol.

The engineer proceeded to try to find out what was the matter with the machine. 'Here you go, this looks interesting,' he said knowingly as he prodded a screwdriver at the circular cover at the back of the machine. 'Somebody's been in here.' He struggled to undo the cover as the screw heads had been damaged by someone using an incorrect tool. Once the cover was off it was easy for the engineer to diagnose the fault. As he and Carol peered into the electronics at the back of the machine, he explained that the timer for the autoclave cycle had been altered, giving a shorter duration and eliminating the cooling phase, and that set as it was the machine wouldn't sterilise. It took him a couple of seconds to rectify the problem, and as Carol signed his paperwork she began to wonder.

Carol took the invoice for the engineer's visit to Dr Davison. She was suprised by the response she got. 'I'm sorry, I'm sorry,' the doctor said. 'It was the easiest thing I could think of at the time.' Carol listened in amazement as Dr Davison admitted that his answer to her request to buy more specula had been to alter the settings on their expensive autoclave in order to shorten the time she would have to wait for the instruments to be ready. She really couldn't believe it.

## Outcome

Dr Davison suggested to Carol Moor that they could sort this out. However, she pointed out that at least three patients had suffered and that there was no way she could cover up for what he had done. After seeking advice from the RCN, Carol discussed the matter with the nurse adviser at her FHSA, who subsequently paid a visit to the practice with the GP adviser.

The FHSA representatives discussed the authority's infection control guidelines with Dr Davison and told him they felt that he had jeopardised safe standards of practice in his surgery and that the matter would have to be taken further, maybe to a service committee hearing.

The three women who contracted infections, together with others Carol thought would be at risk, were contacted by the FHSA and had it explained to them that there had been a fault with the autoclave, although Dr Davison's actions were not mentioned. Carol Moor didn't agree with this approach as she felt that the patients should know the truth; however, the nurse adviser said that Carol had done what was right by informing the FHSA and they would investigate and offer the patients a satisfactory explanation.

## Discussion

I know that this is an extreme case but hopefully we can assume that these sort of things do not happen up and down the country every day. However, this case, which was brought to us by a practice nurse member serves to illustrate the stupid decisions some people can make when the desire to save a little money and inconvenience is put before the safety of patients.

It transpired that Dr Davison was almost bankrupt and could hardly afford petrol for his car, let alone consider buying more specula; the GP adviser explained to him that if he had asked the FHSA for assistance it would have been able to help him out.

Apart from calling the standards of his practice into question and infringing his own code of practice, Dr Davison had broken the law so far as the Health and Safety at Work Act (HSAW) is concerned, in that he put the safety of patients and his staff (Carol Moor) at risk. For example, section 2.1 of HSAW states that:

*'It shall be the duty of every employer to ensure, so far as reasonably practicable, the health, safety and welfare at work of all his employees.'*

And section 2.2(a) continues more specifically to say that:

*'The provision and maintenance of plant and systems of work that are so far as is reasonably practicable, safe and without risks to health...'*

It is obvious that Dr Davison's interference with the autoclave was not the provision of safe plant, and that what he did mitigated against safe systems of work in that they had a potentially deleterious affect on the health of others.

Carol Moor was of course right to refuse to collude in a 'cover up' with the GP. Her code of conduct requires her to do everything within her sphere of responsibility to ensure that no harm comes to her patients. As the nurse adviser pointed out, contacting the FHSA fulfilled this obligation as it was then its responsibility to act, although it is understandable that Carol should be keen for the patients affected to know the truth. It is for the FHSA to investigate the situation and make a report as appropriate, the details of which should be made known to the public concerned.

We could argue that Carol should have been more vigilant in ensuring safe standards of practice for herself. As the sole user of the autoclave she had a responsibility to ensure that it was working properly, and she should have realised that this was not the case. The fact that the instruments were almost too hot to handle should have given her more than a subtle hint that all was not what it should have been. Nevertheless, it was Dr Davison's actions which led to standards of care being jeopardised. He now awaits his fate.

Situations such as this, particularly where there are only one GP and one nurse working together, can be very difficult; however, it is imperative that you stand by your principles and do not get involved in covering up the mistakes of others, no matter how sad the situation may be for those concerned.

## Further reading

Tattam A (1991) Unhygienic practices, (Concerns that vaginal specula are not being properly cleaned). *Nursing Times* **87**(16): 20

Sultan G (1994) Buying an autoclave. *Practice Nursing* **March**: 21

Fuller A (1992) *Journal of Infection Control Nursing*. Sterilising instruments, (Use of portable sterilising equipment in general practice or health centres). *Nursing Times* **88**: 64–5

Harrowing P, Horrex F (1990) Safety before cost. (Safe sterilising of instruments). *Health Service Journal* **100**: 970

See also further reading for case study 9

# Case Study 11
# Practice Nurse Erica Bligh

## Key Issues and Concepts:

- Integrity
- Upholding the good standing and reputation of the profession

Erica Bligh sat behind the desk in her treatment room and briefly surveyed the wall on which all her qualifications were posted in neat hardwood frames. She passed rapidly from her original State Registration certificate (preferring not to remind herself quite how long ago she had received it) to some of the more recent achievements — diplomas in asthma management, nursing and family planning, and her latest, the ENB advanced family planning course.

The neat frames symbolised everything about Erica: her work was tidy and precise, her treatment room was a textbook set-up, in fact the whole practice was orderly and systematic. The building had only been completed 18 months ago, and was fitted out with the most up-to-date equipment. Erica had on her desk a folder of plastic laminated A4 cards which detailed all the main protocols for the practice. Today she had lifted out the card for new patient registrations; she knew this by heart anyway, but always liked to have it in front of her just in case she needed a prompt for her questions. She knew from her regular contact with her GP colleagues that it was important to go through every step in a logical sequence, particularly remembering to check tetanus status, giving a booster to those who were not exactly sure, or who hadn't been immunised in the last five years, and being particularly diligent with the paperwork for new female patients.

Erica recorded all of the new patients' checks in a special book, in addition to making out their new notes; although she didn't have anything to do with it, she knew that the practice manager had to have everything detailed just so in order that the necessary claims could be made to the FHSA.

This particular morning, Erica Bligh had four new patients to see. A young couple who had just moved into the area, and a man and a woman who were coming in individually. As was usually the case for Erica, the consultations went very smoothly, as she followed through the tried and tested practice system. However, her last patient, Elizabeth Andrews, caused something of a 'problem' in that she told Erica her tetanus was up-to-date, even though she did not answer the question as to when she had last been immunised (Erica tried to determine whether this was in the last five years); furthermore, she declined to sign anything there and then, preferring to take everything home to look through it at her leisure. Erica thought this a little odd, but provided Ms Andrews with the necessary paperwork, in particular the form which the GPs and practice manager always insisted new female patients should sign.

Erica diligently wrote up the new patient registration check for the three people whose documentation was complete, and decided to wait until Elizabeth Andrews had returned her forms and brought in her immunisation record card before completing hers. She did not really want to have an entry in the notes which deviated from her usually neat pattern — according to the practice protocol. Erica also knew that the practice manager would not be all that happy about Elizabeth Andrews going off without having completed all the paperwork he needed to 'process' her with the FHSA.

As predicted, the practice manager was a little perturbed that Erica had let a patient deviate from their normal pattern of new patient registrations: 'What if all our patients took everything they were asked to sign home with them?" he said. 'Where would our system be then? As it is, her forms will have a different date from the entry I have made for her on the computer now,' he continued. Erica uttered a hushed 'sorry', and returned to her room.

Erica need not have worried too much, however, as when she came into the practice the next day, the receptionist handed her a telephone message from Elizabeth Andrews, asking that Erica ring her back. Erica still had the beginnings of Ms Andrews' new notes on her desk from the day before, and dialled the number on the front. Ms Andrews sounded quite curt on the phone; then again, thought Erica, she was rather prim and proper in person. Ms Andrews wondered whether Erica would be able to see her that afternoon to discuss the paperwork she had been given, and also she particularly wanted to talk about her family planning needs.

Erica said this would be fine, and as she put the phone down glanced again at her newly acquired family planning certificate. She was so pleased that the partners had seen fit to let her go on the course as she had always worried about giving out advice when she had had no formal training to do so. It was on occasions such as this that she now felt totally confident to deal with every aspect of family planning advice that could possibly be asked of her, or so she thought.

Erica had a busy morning running her travel immunisation clinic, although the fact that the practice had a 'state of the art' computer system which gave details of all injections required, and allowed her to make a record of their administration quickly, did relieve some of the pressure. The day passed quickly, and all that was left was her final appointment with Elizabeth Andrews.

Ms Andrews came into Erica's office (looking even more prim than yesterday). Erica offered her a seat and greeted her with her usual welcoming smile, reiterating their telephone conversation and asking her patient what she could do to help. 'Well, I am particularly interested in the family planning advice you have agreed to give me,' Elizabeth Andrews stated, rather forcibly. This puzzled Erica, as they had not discussed family planning at all; she hesitantly made this point to Ms Andrews. 'This form...' — Ms Andrews produced the FP1001 that she had taken away and waived it in Erica's face. 'This form which you asked me to sign when I was here last. You do know that it relates to you giving me family planning advice don't you?' she retorted. Erica had no chance to reply. As she fumbled for her laminated new patient protocol (the pink one for women), Elizabeth Andrews continued: 'You really expected me to sign all these when we met yesterday, didn't you? I could have been signing anything. As it is you expected me to acknowledge that you were going to help me with planning my family even though I have been trying to get pregnant for the last three years.'

Erica was at a loss. Ms Andrews had never mentioned this at her new patient registration visit; then again she couldn't be sure that she had asked her — it wasn't on her check list after all. Erica had never really read the form that was now being thrust in her face; she just knew it was part of the new registration pack for women, as made up by the practice manager.

## Outcome

Elizabeth Andrews continued to rant and rave, not unsurprisingly, at Erica, who sat behind her desk, almost trying to hide behind her nicely laminated protocol. Eventually Ms Andrews left with the parting words that she would be taking this up with the 'authorities'. Erica was thinking about whether she should mention this to the practice manager, when he came into her office demanding to know what all the noise had been about and why she had upset one of the patients. Having heard Erica's explanation, the practice manager replied with just one four-letter word which should really not grace the pages of this book!

Elizabeth Andrews was true to her word, and the next day Erica found herself hosting a visit from the FHSA nurse adviser. The nurse adviser was actually quite friendly as she elicited from Erica the exact procedure in the practice for undertaking new patient registrations. As diligent as usual, the practice nurse showed her all the protocols, and the nurse adviser had no doubt that an FP1001 form had to be completed for every woman under 50 registering with the practice.

The adviser went on to discuss the immunisation schedules advocated by the practice, as Ms Andrews had also brought up the subject of her tetanus booster, although she had not complained about this to Erica. Again, Erica explained that anyone coming to the practice (not just as a new patient) had to be asked about their tetanus status, and if not immunised within the last five years they had to be given a booster.

As the discussion came to an end, Erica realised that her neat and tidy working practices, with the nicely produced protocols, were not necessarily in the best interests of all her patients. Erica also saw that maybe her practice did not fit in with the current FHSA and Department of Health guidelines on immunisation, and that it was most definitely not acceptable that a claim form for the provision of family planning services should be completed for every woman the practice loosely defined as being of childbearing age, whether or not they utilised those services, or even considered getting pregnant a risk in the first place.

Some time later, the partners in the practice attended a service committee hearing which had been initiated following the enquiry emanating from the nurse adviser's discussion with practice nurse Erica Bligh. While being somewhat more knowledgeable about the rationale behind the practice's strict protocols for new patient registrations than their nurse, the partners did manage to convince the FHSA that they were unaware of the full range of 'income-generating initiatives' (in his own words) that the practice manager had put in place dictating all the 'had to's' in Erica's account of her work.

For example, on investigation the FHSA had found that 60% of patients attending the practice in the last year had been given a tetanus booster, 20 elderly patients who had been given a flu vaccine in October of the preceding year had been invited back in Spring for a 'booster' so that excess stocks could be used up and claimed for, and the practice was giving family planning advice to ten times as many women on its books than any other practice in the area (at least on paper anyway). In addition, 30 of the practice's patients for whom records were still held had died over a year ago, or had duplicate records under other names.

## Discussion

Basically, Erica Bligh fully believed that she had been blessed with a job in an efficient and well-organised practice, which fitted well with her own personal systematic approach to her work. She was well aware of the importance of protocols and was delighted that her practice had been willing to supply her with these on laminated plastic cards in a special binder, making them easy for her to follow.

Unfortunately, Erica's drive for unquestioning efficiency had led her into a situation where she was essentially an accomplice to fraud. Erica should have taken an active part in drawing up the protocols herself. She would then have been able to use all the professional knowledge represented by her wall full of certificates to conclude that while it is acceptable to encourage people to keep vaccinations up to date, and to offer services to those who need it, it is not in the best interests of patients to operate a system where everyone gets everything unless they say otherwise.

Erica Bligh's entrapment in such a system is by no means unique. The RCN has many enquiries from practice nurses who have unearthed dead patients (so to speak) and been told to keep quiet about it, or have been told to disregard accepted immunisation schedules or complete spurious documentation for the sake of profit. Nurses must refuse to compromise their principles, as they not only risk potential criminal prosecution, but are also likely to convince their profession that they were not acting in a manner which upholds and enhances its image, or doing the best for their patients, as required by the *Code of Professional Conduct*.

In this particular example the practice manager also believed that he had done no wrong. He had come from a large city accountancy firm and single-mindedly set about maximising the practice's profit margin within what he considered to be the rules of the game. Perhaps the actions of such individuals, some GPs, and even some practice nurses can be excused to a certain extent by the fact that general practice is increasingly being made to operate as a small business in a health-care market, but such actions are not those of a professional dedicated to bringing the best in health care to their patients. Think carefully before you get involved in the numbers game.

# Further reading

UKCC (1993) *Standards for Records and Record Keeping.* UKCC, London

# Case Study 12
# Practice Nurses Amanda Taylor and Alison Richards

## Key Issues and Concepts:

- Expanded role
- Scope of Professional Practice
- Holistic care

Amanda Taylor and Alison Richards, worked in a newly approved fund-holding practice. The GP partners there all had a variety of specialist interests which they almost followed as a 'hobby' alongside their day-to-day consultations. These interests ranged from sports medicine, through acupuncture, to genitourinary medicine.

The partners felt that fund-holding now offered them an ideal opportunity to develop their special interests into commercially viable propositions, offering a range of specialised services to their colleagues in the area, local business, etc. Already Dr Harrison had begun to negotiate a contract with the nearby university, where he also engaged in research, to offer a service to all the players on their various teams (football, rugby, swimming, athletics, etc.) based around his work on sports injury.

Spurred on by their colleague, and not wanting to be left out of it, the other partners desperately searched for ways and means to promote their own particular interest as a practice income generator. It comes as no suprise, therefore, that the practice nurses were soon seen by all as being crucial to their plans. It was also obvious to Amanda and Alison that they must adopt a common stance to ensure that they didn't get pulled in all directions and end up running dozens of new clinics just to keep up with their employers' passions. They had had enough of that with the old-style health promotion clinics. At least with the banding system they were now able to plan their work with some degree of rationality, rather than just engaging in what Amanda used to call 'bums on seats health promotion'.

The practice nurses agreed together that they would meet the doctors and let them know that they were prepared to assist with two new clinics for now, just to see how they went, as this was all they could manage with their existing workload. As Dr Harrison's sports injury clinic was almost up and running already they would do this one (particularly as the suggested trips to the university to see the players sounded an interesting diversion from new patient registrations and over-75 checks). They would let the doctors decide among themselves which of their other schemes the nurses would be engaged in, and if they wanted them to do more then they would have to look at altering the practice nurses' current workload.

Amanda and Alison were also acutely aware, after all they had read, that they would need to consider their experience, and whether or not they would require any extra training in order to do whatever the doctors had in mind for them in these new clinics.

At the next practice meeting, the practice nurses took the initiative to discuss the proposals for the sports injury clinic, and any others the partners had in mind. The GPs were quite used to Amanda and Alison making presentations detailing what could or could not be expected of them, and were receptive to this approach. Essentially this was because, in addition to Alison and Amanda being well read on the subject of professional accountability, a GP in a neighbouring practice had been suspended six months previously as a result of an allegation that he had forced his practice nurse to undertake work for which she was neither trained nor competent. The general feeling of 'there but for the grace of God go I' was still in the air for the GPs, and even though Alison and Amanda never felt they had been placed in such a situation they thought it quite legitimate to capitalise on the partners' new found attitude of heightened responsibility.

At the meeting, the partners eventually came to an agreement that they would pilot Dr Harrison's sports injury programme, together with Dr Doogan's genitourinary clinic. The nurses did not really understand the raised eyebrows of the other partners, let alone the stage-whispered comment from Dr Hart, the other partner, 'This should be interesting!' he said with a grin.

As with most cases, my involvement with Amanda Taylor and Alison Richards began with a telephone call to the RCN asking for some advice. Amanda placed the call and wanted to know whether the College's indemnity insurance would cover them to undertake cryosurgery. I said that it would and explained the need to be competent to practise, for proper education etc; Amanda was quite reassuring, managing to quote back at me parts of *The Scope of Professional Practice* document which were locked temporarily in the recesses of my mind. Nevertheless, we had quite an interesting discussion and Amanda promised to send me some more details of their proposed clinics.

At the end of November, Amanda was true to her word, and a letter arrived containing an interesting document relating to Dr Harrison's sports injury clinic, with the protocols that were being used; however, this was nothing like as interesting as the information relating to Dr Doogan's clinics. There was a letter, which had presumably been circulated to other GPs, containing selected highlights such as 'The Beauchamp practice now offers a sophisticated genitourinary service, specialising in the removal of anal warts and skin tags using the latest in cryosurgical techniques. Our practice nurses have been trained to the highest standard and are able to tailor the service to the exact requirements of your patients...' and so it went on.

Now, on a cold winter's day huddled in my office at the RCN, this did raise some interest. I don't know whether I was more intrigued as to how the practice would generate sufficient business in the anal wart line to keep the nurses busy, or to how Amanda and Alison would set about 'tailoring the service to individual requirements'. As I would be driving almost past the Beauchamp practice on my way to visit relatives for Christmas, I arranged with Amanda to call in and see how their clinic operated for myself (as an observer not a participant).

## Outcome

On arrival at the practice I thought that I had walked into something from the 21st century. The architecture was striking and the interior a mix of brushed chrome and natural wood, with a couple of video monitors built into the wall giving out health messages. The practice leaflet scattered on the smoked glass coffee tables was in fact a practice book crammed with details of the services on offer, not least the anal wart clinic (although it was described here as the genitourinary clinic 'for patients with particular personal needs' — what was this meant to be about?)

Amanda and Alison were two of the most pleasant and enthusiastic practice nurses I had ever met. First, they talked me through the sports clinic and we discussed the care provided with the captain of the university first fifteen who had just finished seeing the practice physiotherapist. The clinic seemed to be going really well, with the nurses working as integral members of the health-care team. However, when we moved to the other clinic, things were a little different.

I rapidly came to see why Dr Hart had remarked on the potential 'interest' of Dr Doogan's specialty. Basically the two nurses were seeing patient after patient in this clinic with either anal warts or peri-anal skin tags which they treated with a cryoprobe. These nurses were anal wart zappers — period!

Amanda and Alison had done all their *Code of Professional Conduct* required of them, and complied with their interpretation of *The Scope of Professional Practice* and my advice about ensuring that they were competent. Their knowledge of anal warts, I am sure, was unparalleled. They could describe every manifestation of the condition and the best probe to use to 'get at the sneaky ones' (Alison's words), and they knew all about every cryosurgical instrument on the market and its benefits and drawbacks. They could describe the seemingly unnecessarily complicated system of ordering liquid nitrogen, and the storage and handling of the stuff on the practice premises. But I had to ask: 'What about patient care?' The two of them looked puzzled.

## Discussion

What I had seen in the Beauchamp practice was a picture of stark contrasts. On the one hand, Amanda Taylor and Alison Richards were part of a comprehensive health-care team running a sports injury clinic which was practice based with a novel outreach service to the university campus — excellent work. On the other, I saw two practice nurses whose concept of holistic nursing care had been replaced with the single-minded proficiency of a production-line worker, ultraskilled in one area — in this case treating an anal wart with a cryoprobe — with no concern for what happened to the component, i.e. a patient, either before it reached them or when it had moved away down the assembly line.

In their enthusiasm to set up and run the clinic, Amanda and Alison had become absorbed in the technology of cryosurgery and its application to a specific area of treatment. There was no doubt that they were specialists, but they had forgotten that they were nurses caring for a whole patient. The protocols they used, and the consequent interaction they had with patients, gave no opportunity for discussing the history of each individual's problems, their aftercare, or strategies for maintaining their health in the future. The nurses had become so caught up with the business of treating a wart that they had almost forgotten there was a person attached to it.

In drafting *The Scope of Professional Practice*, the UKCC was mindful of the possibility of nurses expanding their role in a similar way to Amanda and Alison. There have already been widely discussed cases, such as that of the nurse employed as a surgeon's assistant, in which role expansion had taken place, but potentially to the detriment of nursing practice. The *Scope* guidance is quite clear in this respect:

> '...*any enlargement or adjustment of the scope of personal professional practice must be achieved without compromising or fragmenting existing aspects of professional practice and care and that the requirements of the Council's* Code of Professional Conduct *are satisfied throughout the whole area of practice...*'

(UKCC, 1992, section 9.4)

*The Scope of Professional Practice* does indeed give nursing a new-found freedom, in that we are now able to expand practice within the boundaries of our own predetermined competencies, without having to rely on the sanction of other professional groups. However, it is vital that when role expansion is considered we do not fall into the same trap as Amanda Taylor and Alison Richards. It is right and proper to develop a nursing expertise in a specific clinical area, but we must not lose sight of the fact that first and foremost we are nurses, and our forte is being able to offer a comprehensive package of care, considering the total needs of our patients and clients, not just one specific problem that they may be experiencing at a particular moment in time. These principles hold true whenever a patient attends the surgery, whether it be for a travel vaccination, a cervical smear, or whatever. It is all too easy to focus on one body system or one particular problem when faced with a seemingly continual stream of patients, but nursing values must come first, not those of the production line.

## References

UKCC (1992) *The Scope of Professional Practice*. UKCC, London

## Further reading

Mechanic HF (1988) Redefining the expanded role. *Nursing Outlook* **36**(6): 280–4

Richards S (1991) A fast expanding role: developments in practice nursing, *Professional Nurse* **6**(9): 550, 552–3

Tredinnick B (1991) Put into practice, (Expanding role of the practice nurse). *Nursing Times* **87**(49): 19

Winter M (1994) Hope, scope and a jump. (Nurses should embrace the opportunities to extend their role by the increasing scope of professional practice). *Nursing Standard* **8**(40): 53

Wright S (1989) In camera: expanding the nurse's role. *Nursing Standard* **3**(36): 44

See also further reading for Chapter 3

# Case Study 13
# Practice Nurse Maria Forster

## Key Issues and Concepts:

• Consent

• Administration of Medicines

• Negligence

Practice Nurse Maria Forster was determined to start the week ahead of the paperwork — for once — and had managed to drag herself into the surgery at the unearthly hour of 8.00 am, certainly for a Monday morning. Nobody else was in the building and just as she gazing out of the window thinking to herself that she must be mad coming in at this time, Dr Malcolm's weary old Jaguar trundled into the car park. 'Why didn't he get a new car?' she thought, although she knew his answer would be the usual 'I love that car like a good woman; you wouldn't want to be traded in just because you were getting a little rough round the edges, would you now, Maria?'

A few minutes later, looking almost as weary as the vehicle from which he slowly clambered, Dr Malcolm plodded toward the surgery door. He was nearing his retirement and suffered from rheumatism badly, yet Maria couldn't help thinking that his gait had deteriorated somewhat over the weekend. Anyway, the doctor's arrival spurred her into action, and Maria gathered up her notes for the series of elderly assessments she had lined up for the morning. She was quite pleased that the elderly population on their list was pretty active, and well over three-quarters of the over-75s chose to come into the practice, so saving her the bother of visiting them at home.

Maria's second patient of the day was Alfred Adams. Mr Adams still ran a farm with his twin brother, although as they were both nearing eighty, their four sons did most of the work. Alfred was an interesting character, and Maria had got to know him quite well following an accident he had had a couple of years ago. He was mixing some fertiliser solution, when the pressurised container leaked, sending an aerosol of the fluid over his arms and chest. Mr Adams got over this reasonably well, the only remaining problem being acute sensitivity of the skin and underlying tissue in the areas he had burned.

Alfred came into the consulting room with his usual warm greeting for Maria, which included a kiss on the cheek, from which she knew she would develop a spontaneous urticaria as a result of the mixture of two-day-old stubble and aftershave of rather dubious provenance. The check went fine, and all that was left was to give the farmer his scheduled flu vaccine. Maria explained to Alfred that because of his past injuries she would give the injection in his behind, as she had done previously, as this was the least painful option for him.

Mr Adams leant across the examination couch, and mumbled a series of barely audible expletives, which did nothing for Maria's concentration. In fact, as she removed the cover from the vaccine she managed to bend the needle. Her curse added to those of Mr Adams, particularly as she had only brought one vial into the room with her, and the rest of the supply was upstairs in the drugs fridge. She explained the problem to her patient, who thankfully replied 'never you mind lass, I'll just lean over 'ere wi' me trousers down me ankles till yer gets back; just be quick about it mind!'

Maria dashed upstairs to the drugs fridge and hurriedly selected another flu vaccine. She ran back down the stairs, popping the cover of the needle as she burst through the door of the consulting room. She smirked to herself as she saw the elderly gent's bottom 'staring' up at her, but quickly set about the task in hand. 'I'm back', she announced. 'Just a small prick now.' She anticipated that Mr Adams would make a fuss, as he always did, but she wasn't ready for the reply which came: 'What in the name of ...', the patient yelled, but that voice didn't sound like Mr Adams. 'What do you think you are doing woman?' Dr Malcolm bellowed as he turned to face the nurse, his trousers draped around his ankles. Maria was speechless, and could only manage to jabber an incoherent reply, faced with the spectacle of the semi-clad doctor resplendent before her.

## Outcome

It dawned on Maria what had happened. The practice had four consulting rooms, all exactly the same but numbered differently; the practice nurses and GPs simply used the one that was free at the time. At the foot of the stairs down which Maria had dashed were the doors to two of the rooms. She had left Mr Adams in consulting room 2, to the left of the stairs, but had inadvertently gone into room 3, to the right. Unknown to Maria, poor Dr Malcolm's ponderous gait that morning had been the result of a flare up of his haemorrhoids over the weekend. He had sought some relief through the application of a proprietary cream, and had chosen to apply this in the consulting room, not thinking to lock the door. Unfortunately for him, his rheumatism had got the better of him and he was stuck leaning over the couch. A jab in the backside from Maria did the trick and got him mobile again, but it was not the solution the doctor had desired.

Maria remembered Mr Adams and mumbled an apology to the doctor before somehow managing to get another vaccine and administer it to the right person. After she had tended to the needs of her real patient, Maria was summoned to the presence of her inadvertent one. Dr Malcolm was most displeased with the practice nurse's actions, and had by now had a chance to mull over the fact that she had seen him standing with his trousers around his ankles, let alone stuck a hypodermic needle into his rear. Accordingly, the doctor told Maria Forster that her actions were most unbecoming from one of his nurses and that he felt that their professional relationship could never be the same again. He asked her to leave the practice that day, with a month's pay in lieu of her due period of notice.

## Discussion

Funny as this account might seem, there are a number of lessons to be learnt concerning privacy for patients, consent to treatment, and general organisation. First, even though Alfred Adams seemed happy enough to stay draped over the consulting room couch, Maria should not have left him like this, even if only for a couple of minutes, especially as there was no apparent means of locking the door. At the very least there should have been some form of 'engaged' sign available. Maria Forster should have noted clause 11 of the UKCC *Code of Professional Conduct* which advises nurses to:

> '...*report to an appropriate person or authority, having regard to the physical, psychological and social effects on patients and clients, any circumstances in the environment of care which could jeopardise standards of practice;*'

Bearing this in mind, Maria should have ensured that Mr Adams' privacy could not have been compromised, and might well have questioned whether she should have left him as she did. In addition, clause 11 gives the nurse the basis to request that provision should be made for facilities such as locks on doors or engaged signs.

Also, simply asking Mr Adams (or as we now know — Dr Malcolm) whether he was ready for his injection, and leaving time for a reply, would have ensured that the vaccine was not put into the wrong bottom. It is always worth reaffirming consent just before administration of an injection. Above all, Maria should have been more organised, perhaps having a spare vaccine available should it be needed, not running up and down the stairs (which would not have been necessary if she had not been worrying about leaving the patient in such a compromising position), and not preparing the vaccine as she ran through the door of the consulting room. Another obvious point is that she should have remembered which consulting room she had left Mr Adams in.

Finally, what of the actions of Dr Malcolm? It was his surgery, and so he had a legitimate right to use the consulting room for his self-medication, yet he also should have taken steps to ensure that no-one could enter the room. What if a patient had walked in to be met by the sight of his bare posterior? He was right in one thing: Maria Forster's injecting him with the flu vaccine could be construed as an assault. Although he would have to demonstrate that he had been harmed by her actions, he could well win some damages from her. The doctor could also have reported the nurse to the UKCC, for what was certainly an unprofessional action.

At the end of the day, he did not, and with a little intervention from the RCN came to see the funny side of the matter. Locks and proper signs were fitted to the consulting room doors, and they were also painted different colours so that even the most harassed individual would have a better chance of remembering which room the patient was in. Alfred Adams returned home, none the wiser regarding his role in providing Dr Malcolm with a flu injection, but perhaps wondering why the nurse left him bottom-up for quite as long as she did.

# Reference

UKCC (1992) *Standards for the Administration of Medicines*. UKCC, London

# Further reading

As for case study 1

# Case Study 14
# Practice Nurse Nerys Davies

## Key Issues and Concepts:

- *The Scope of Professional Practice*/expanded roles
- Midwifery care in general practice

Practice nurse Nerys Davies was looking forward to the day's work. She especially liked Wednesdays as this was the day that Dr Evans ran his ante-natal clinic. It was actually Nerys' clinic, as Dr Evans had little to do with it, unless of course she felt that a patient needed to see him specifically. Nerys was particularly proud of being able to manage the clinic by herself, and that the doctor was able to acknowledge her ability in this way. She found great satisfaction in seeing her patients before and after delivery, and meeting the 'little ones' who were the practice population of tomorrow. In fact she wished that more patients would transfer their care to the practice completely, rather than sharing the care with St Margaret's Hospital in town. After all, her ladies were always complaining to her that it was something of a trek from their little village, and that the midwives in the hospital didn't really have time for the personal touch.

Nerys Davies was adamant that the least she could do was make the ante-natal visits to the practice as pleasant as possible. She thought herself particularly lucky in that she had both an office and a treatment room to herself, and had chosen the decor for the latter, which was homely yet still exuded an air of clinical efficiency. She felt that the restful tones of the wallpaper and the pastel shade blinds were particularly suited to the antenatal clinic, and she knew that they also had a relaxing effect on women coming in for smears. She did occasionally wonder what her male patients made of it, but then why shouldn't they be treated to a little tranquillity as well.

Today wasn't too busy; only six women were booked in for the clinic and Nerys would have plenty of time to chat with them if they had any problems or questions. The first patient of the day was Emily Jones. Emily was pregnant with her second child which was due in 11 weeks time. Nerys was glad to see Emily as she was an experienced mum and never had any real difficulties; it would be good to chat with her. As Nerys predicted, Emily was getting on just fine, although she did say that James (her scan had confirmed that she was having a boy, and he had already been given a name, although Nerys thought this was a little strange) had been a little quieter than of late. Apparently James had definite periods of restfulness, but over the past couple of days Emily had hardly felt him at all.

Nerys took her 'trumpet' down from the shelf and pressed it against Emily's bulging abdomen. The patient reacted to her frown: 'Is there a problem?' she asked. 'No, not really,' the practice nurse replied. 'It's just that I can't quite hear his little heartbeat, but not to worry — you can't always hear it you know.' Emily Jones commented that when she goes

133

to clinics at St Margaret's, they generally listen to James' heart through one of those 'electric microphones'. 'Ah yes,' said Nerys, 'That would be a sonogram or something like that — it's an ultrasonic thing. But they cost hundreds and we haven't got one in the surgery.' Despite the practice nurse's assurances, Emily was concerned that James' heartbeat could not be detected, and eventually Nerys had to admit that the services at the hospital were superior, and suggested that Emily might want to pop in and let them try.

The only problem with this was that Emily's partner was away on business until Friday, and she had no way of getting into town. She didn't relish the thought of an hour each way on the dilapidated buses — not in her condition. In her usual way, Nerys managed to calm her patient down and established that her partner would be phoning home that evening, and suggested that Emily might ask him to come home a day early so that they could both pop down to the hospital together. Emily Jones, looking a little calmer now, agreed with the nurse, chatted for a few more minutes, and left. Nerys sat and wondered for a few minutes, then reassured herself that Emily and James would be just fine; she complimented herself on being able to calm Emily and help her to see reason.

## Outcome

Emily did indeed speak to her husband that evening, and in doing so became rather anxious again. He was so worried that he said he would set off home that evening, then they could go to the hospital first thing. The next day a tired Emily and husband (he got home at 3.00 am) set off for the hospital, after calling to let the antenatal clinic know they were on their way. Once in the clinic, Emily thought how 'sterile' it felt compared with the surgery, but she felt better about this when she spied the 'electronic microphone' in the midwife's hand. Although she felt at ease with Nerys Davies, Emily felt more relaxed knowing that St Margaret's could afford the technology needed for her to hear her son's heartbeat.

The midwife switched on the machine, and blobbed the cold gel onto Emily's bump, and with the usual 'swooshing' sound moved it around listening for the beat. However, Emily noticed the same frown on the midwife's face as had been present on the practice nurse's. Her panic heightened when the midwife went off to find a colleague as she too was unable to locate James' heartbeat. The first midwife then returned with a doctor who was carrying a bigger version of the machine the midwives were using. The swooshes were louder, but still no beat. Emily began to cry as the doctor said they would have to admit her into the hospital for observation.

Only the next day, a desperately upset Emily Jones was recovering from the therapeutic abortion of her dead son. Even though everyone talked of the 'fetus' she felt that she had know James for ages, and that he was a real person who she would never see. The obstetrician told Emily there was no indication that anything had been going wrong with her pregnancy, and that all her previous antenatal tests had been satisfactory, as were the reports from her practice. The only way of telling what had happened to James would be to conduct a postmortem. After much discussion with her husband, Emily decided she would oppose this, and informed the doctor that she did not want her baby examined in this way. Although the obstetrician believed this to be highly irregular, he agreed with her wishes.

Sometime later that day, a very distressed Nerys Davies visited her patient in hospital. They both cried and cried, and eventually Nerys sobbed 'if only I could have done something.'

## Discussion

Practice nurse Nerys Davies was obviously a very caring person. She had given due regard to the environment of care in her practice, and gone out of her way to ensure that the patients attending her antenatal clinic were put at ease. But herein lies the problem: Nerys was a practice nurse — not a midwife — and yet she was in effect running an ante-natal clinic. Should Dr Evans have been more involved, given the lack of his nurse's midwifery skills?

It is acceptable for a GP operating a shared-care antenatal programme to delegate aspects of that antenatal care to a midwife, but in entrusting a practice nurse with no formally recognised skills with this work, he had clearly omitted to determine whether or not she was competent to accept such delegation. Furthermore, while some practice nurses weigh patients, test urine, and measure blood pressure at antenatal clinics, and it could be argued that as registered nurses they are competent to do so, to go as far as Nerys Davies and to attempt to listen to fetal sounds and give advice about the pregnancy clearly moves into the domain of midwifery practice.

The same Act of Parliament which brought into being the UKCC, and resulted in the publication of the *Code of Professional Conduct* — the Nurses, Midwives and Health Visitors Act 1979 (see Chapter 2) — also requires that the UKCC makes rules regulating the practice of midwifery. The Midwives Rules (UKCC, 1993) require any midwife intending to practise to give notice of that intention every year. Clearly Nerys Davies could not do this as she was not on part 10 of the professional register — she was not a registered midwife and did not fulfil the criteria to qualify as a 'practising midwife'. Specifically, the 1979 Act makes it an offence for anyone to falsely represent themselves as included on any part of the register when they are not.

These provisions override any concept of expanded roles under the auspices of the guidelines within *The Scope of Professional Practice* (see Chapter 3), in that midwifery is defined specifically by the UKCC and requires a specific registration for practice.

At the time of writing, no complaint has been received from Emily Jones about the actions of her practice nurse. If she had chosen to take some action, then a complaint to the UKCC could have resulted in a charge of professional misconduct against the nurse; it was a fact that she was practising midwifery without relevant qualifications and registration. Emily could try to seek some recompense through the civil courts, arguing that Nerys was negligent in her work. This could be a little more problematic, as she would have to prove that the nurse's care led to her being harmed in some way (see Chapter 5). If Nerys couldn't hear the fetal heartbeat then it was likely the baby was already dead, and her advice to call into the hospital when Emily's partner had returned from the business trip would have made little difference. If Emily had waited, say a week, based on the nurse's advice, things may well have been different.

Through negotiation with Dr Evans and his representative organisation, it was resolved that Nerys Davies should no longer provide any services as part of the practice's antenatal programme. The GP had not realised that it was not appropriate for him to delegate this work to his practice nurse, even though this is explained in clear guidance from the General Medical Council (GMC), which requires all medical practitioners to ensure that whoever they delegate work to is competent to accept that delegation (GMC, 1995). The practice was soon to become part of a non-fundholding consortium, and through that grouping, midwives would be used to provide an effective antenatal service.

Nerys was upset as losing a pleasurable part of her work, but she would have been a good deal more upset at losing her registration as a nurse. If you are at all involved in antenatal work consider carefully where the line should be drawn between your practice as a nurse, and that of a midwife. The penalties for crossing that line can be grave, not only for you but also for your patients.

## References

General Medical Council (1995) *Duties of a Doctor*, (Paragraph 28). GMC, London

UKCC (1993). *Midwives Rules*. UKCC, London

## Further reading

Dimond B (1993) Client autonomy and choice, (Legal implications for midwives). *Modern Midwife* 3(1): 15–6

Dimond B (1994) GPs, maternity medical services and midwives, (Legal aspects of maternity services provided by GPs). *Modern Midwife* 4(7): 32—3

# Case Study 15
# Practice Nurse Lisa Turner

## Key Points and Concepts:

- Breach of confidentiality in the wider public interest
- Respect for privileged access to patient's property
- The offer of gifts

Lisa Turner cursed under her breath; she found it difficult getting up and out for work at the best of times, without that wretched toaster burning the bread each morning. Anyway, her birthday was coming up soon and she could add a replacement to her 'hint list', boring as that may seem. A couple of cups of coffee and a slice of scraped burnt toast later, Lisa was flying out of her flat and down to the surgery for another busy day.

The morning's clinics went by just fine, and after a reasonable lunch — no burnt bits this time — Lisa Turner was all set to do some over-75 visits and a couple of flu jabs for people who couldn't get to the surgery. At least she could go out and get a breath of fresh air, Lisa thought.

The last visit of the afternoon was to 78-year-old Mrs Jacobs. She lived in a rambling old house at the far end of a country lane. Fortunately her son and daughter-in-law were nearly always there, even though they didn't live with the old lady. As she expected, Lisa's knock at the door was met by Mrs Jacobs' cheery son Alan, who asked her in. 'Mum's in the front room if you want to go through,' Alan said. 'Cup of tea do you?' Lisa was a little taken aback as she went into the living room: her patient was sat in a high-backed chair in one corner, with a big welcoming smile, but to get to her the nurse had to walk down a virtual corridor of — 'Well, what were they?' she thought. 'Why, they're toasters — dozens of them!'

Lisa took her mind off the irony of being surrounded by toasters piled to the ceiling, given the fraught start to her day caused by her own deviant appliance, and concentrated on giving Mrs Jacobs her flu jab. Alan returned with her tea, and seeing her at the end of the toaster tunnel, apologised for the state of the room. Lisa explained that she saw the funny side and related the story of her burnt bread. 'Oh, right,' said Alan, 'just take one on your way out if you want.' With that, he left the room. Lisa asked Mrs Jacobs if it was OK for her to go through to the kitchen to wash her hands — no problem. The practice nurse moved through the house in sheer amazement; what she remembered as an empty old place was literally stuffed full of boxes. The walk through the hallway to the kitchen entailed her passing ten or so colour TVs and what looked like three piles of CD players or some form of hi-fi equipment wrapped in cellophane. Lisa washed her hands and returned to Mrs Jacobs. Finding it a little difficult to contain her curiosity she asked her patient what her son did for a living: 'Nothing just now dear, he's unemployed, but he is looking for a job.' Lisa managed to make her excuses to Mrs Jacobs who was now in full flow about the vagaries of Government employment policy (no need to test her mental ability for a 75+ check), and shouting a goodbye to Alan, she set off back to the surgery.

As she drove, Lisa remembered that she had forgotten to take a toaster, but as soon as she realised this, her previously unconscious thoughts popped out: 'what if they're nicked?' she thought, and laughed to herself out loud. 'Maybe I should have told Alan that my TV and stereo had packed in as well. I could have had replacements loaded in the back of the car by now.' Lisa was only joking to herself, but she soon began to wonder whether she should tell anyone.

Back at the practice, Lisa approached one of the younger partners, Dr Siddely, and asked whether she could discuss something in confidence. The doctor gave his assurances and Lisa related the story of Mrs. Jacobs emporium of electrical goods. 'Well, it's not really anything to do with us, is it Lisa?' was his first response. 'But I do have Mac Roberts coming in tomorrow to talk about some of the area's drug problems. I could mention it to him if you like?' Mac Roberts was the local community police officer. The practice got on quite well with him since he helped them through a bad time when computer equipment had been stolen. He was now working quite closely with Dr Siddely on setting up a drug information project. Lisa thanked her colleague for his advice, but said that she would deal with the situation herself.

The next morning, Lisa Turner hadn't given much thought to the toaster issue; her own functioned normally for once. That was until her phone rang and the receptionist told her that Mrs Jacbobs' son, Alan, was on the phone. In the split second after asking him to be put through and him speaking, Lisa's thoughts skittered between thinking he was ringing to remind her to pick up the toaster, and the possibility that he now realised she had been a witness to his horde and was ringing to put the 'frighteners' on. Actually Alan said that his mother was not feeling all that well since her injection and could she come along to see her. Lisa thought about bottling out and asking the district nurse to visit, but she had given the flu jab, and she should follow it up. Anyway, it would give her the opportunity to nose around a bit more.

Back at the Jacobs' house, Alan let the practice nurse in. Mrs Jacobs was sat in her chair again and did indeed look a little lethargic. On examination she was running a slight temperature, and Lisa determined she was suffering from the after-affects of the injection. Just as she was glancing around at the toaster maze once again, the phone rang, and she could just about make out the ensuing conversation between Alan and whoever was at the other end.

Even though Alan spoke in hushed tones, Lisa clearly made out the words: 'What are the jellies going for?' and 'Not bad, we can knock them out to the kids at St Hugh's and down the station for five times that.' Alan finished the conversation with 'OK, get him to meet us outside The Birch at two o'clock; we'll pick them up then, and start getting them out on the street tonight.' Lisa was ready to leave, but wondered whether Alan had forgotten she was there; what would his reaction be when she poked her head around the door? She had nothing to fear as Alan walked into the room and quietly asked how his mother was. Mustering all her capacity for a nonchalant reply, Lisa explained that she thought his mother was just having a mild reaction to the flu jab, and if she did not get any better towards the end of the day he should ring the surgery.

Driving to the surgery this time, all Lisa was no longer concerned about toasters and TV sets. She was totally convinced that she had heard Alan making a drugs deal, she knew where the transaction was to take place, and most galling she knew who the drugs were destined for — children at the local middle school, and those scruffy teenagers who hang about at the station all day.

## Outcome

Arriving back at the surgery, Lisa asked the receptionist whether Dr Siddely was still in his meeting. He was, and Lisa went in to see him. Her revelations certainly put a different perspective on Mac Roberts' agenda for the day so far as targeting the area's drug problems were concerned. Over the next two hours, Lisa made a statement at the police station, and sat in the back of an unmarked police car to identify Alan Jacobs waiting outside The Birch public house, literally yards from the practice premises.

Mac Roberts visited Lisa and Dr Siddely at the practice the following day. It turned out that the nurse's suspicions were right. Alan Jacobs and his friend had been buying and selling on stolen temazepam capsules (jellies) for some months, and her observations had allowed the police to catch them red-handed.

Lisa Turner was required to give evidence against Alan in court — a harrowing experience — but she thought it was worth it. She was a little upset that she had caused the son of one of her favourite patients to be sent to prison. Even though Mrs Jacobs never mentioned her son or the incident when Lisa saw her subsequently, she wondered what she thought; after all, Lisa would never have found anything out if she hadn't been visiting Mrs Jacobs at home. In the long run Lisa believed she had done the right thing. She knew that she had helped to remove a menace from the streets.

## Discussion

It is obvious that I have selected this case study to consider one aspect of the issue of confidentiality, so far as accountability to our patients is concerned. You will remember that clause 10 of the *Code of Professional Conduct* specifically states that in exercising professional accountability, nurses must:

> *'...protect all confidential information concerning patients and clients obtained in the course of professional practice and make disclosures only with consent, where required by the order of a court or where you can justify disclosure in the wider public interest;'*

Lisa Turner was therefore faced with a situation in which she had obtained information by virtue of the fact that her patient's son was engaged in criminal activity, and this had come to her attention as a result of providing care to that patient. She had to decide whether she was required to say nothing, based on the need to restrict confidential information, or to provide information to the police based on her assessment that it was in the wider public interest.

In its elaborated guidance on aspects of the *Code* — Ethical Guidelines for Professional Practice — the UKCC (1996) states that:

*'...confidentiality should only be broken in exceptional circumstances and should only occur after careful consideration that you can justify to yourself;'*

Lisa Turner was in a situation where she had to make a decision; how could she be sure it was the right one?

On the face of it this may seem pretty straightforward, but consider also clause 9 of the *Code*:

*'...avoid any abuse of your privileged relationship with patients and clients and of the privileged access allowed to their person, property residence, or workplace;'*

Based on clause 10 alone, Lisa Turner could justify passing on the information about Alan relatively easily. The information was nothing to do with her patient, Mrs Jacobs, or her care; it concerned a third party who was not connected with the care being given. However, clause 9 reminds us that we should not abuse the fact that access to a patient's home is a privilege. Could this imply that as Lisa only found out about Alan's drug dealing because his mother's need for care allowed her access to the home, passing on information about him gained in this way would be contrary to this stipulation?

Essentially, Lisa came to the decision that disclosing the information about Alan was in the wider public interest, and knowing that there was a drug problem in the area, and that the outlet for the drugs he was to buy included children at the local school, she felt able to justify this decision. Even if Alan had been Lisa's patient, and she had overhead the same conversation, she could still be justified in putting the potential risk to the health of the wider community before the need to maintain confidentiality.

This last point is particularly relevant. If Lisa had decided to tell the police about the electrical equipment, would her reasoning be as easily justified? Perhaps not. The fact that Alan may or may not have stolen the toasters, TVs or whatever did not have the same bearing on the wider public interest as the drug deal. If Alan had been the patient, rather than his mother, and Lisa chose to tell about the goods, she would clearly have taken advantage of his position as a patient to obtain that information, and justifying her actions could be difficult. As an aside, if she had taken the toaster offered, having admitted to herself that it could have been stolen, Lisa would certainly have been in breach of her *Code of Professional Conduct* (see the discussion in Chapter 3 referring to the four guiding principles of the *Code*).

The UKCC emphasises that the disclosure of confidential information obtained during the course of professional practice should be an exception, and when such disclosure takes place the practitioner should have good grounds. Lisa Turner's action in this case was appropriate, and drug trafficking is particularly highlighted by the UKCC as being a situation where a nurse should act in the wider public interest (UKCC, 1996).

It is useful to consider how you might act when faced with such a situation. If you do find yourself in such a dilemma, take stock of the situation, talk it through with colleagues, and seek advice from your professional organisation as appropriate. Lisa Turner did not have the luxury of time to make her decision as the drug deal was going down in a matter of hours; preparation for such an event will help, should it happen to you.

## References

UKCC (1996) *Ethical Guidelines for Professional Practice*. UKCC, London

## Further reading

Young A (1991) Exerting undue influence, (Legal problems of nurses accepting gifts). *Nursing Standard* 5(20): 8–19

# Case Study 16
# Practice Nurse Totty Maize

## Key Issues and Concepts:

- The need to safeguard patient interests at all costs
- The requirement to report bad practice
- The pressure and stress faced by 'whistleblowers'

Seeing that her working day should have ended an hour and a half ago, practice nurse Totty Maize left the practice for the weekend, filled with a mixed emotion of dedication to the cause and feeling that she was being put upon. She knew, though, that the extra work was well worth it, as two of the partners were away on a convention for the whole of the next week, and were only going to be replaced by one locum. Having the place tidy, with everything in the right place, was the least she could do to ensure that she didn't get tripped up by the inevitably increased workload that was to come.

Monday morning came around all too soon, yet Totty managed to get into the surgery early, to be sure that she was there before the locum arrived. She wanted to be there first; he was a guest in her practice, and she felt that he needed to see that. Totty's initial scepticism that any locum could replace the two colleagues with whom she had worked for years was overcome within minutes of meeting Dr Manley ('call me David'). He was a tall elegant man, quite handsome in fact, and he cut quite a dash in his three-piece suit and spotted bow tie. Totty Maize reminded herself that while he might look and appear all right, this was no indicator of his ability to get through their usual Monday morning crowd. She would reserve judgment.

Somewhat surprisingly the morning went well. The two remaining GPs, Totty and her colleague managed perfectly well with the help of David Manley. 'This afternoon will be different,' thought the unusually negative Totty. 'Well-woman clinic — that'll get him.' We should note at this point that ordinarily Totty Maize was quite a caring individual who enjoyed working in the practice team, but certain factors had conspired which caused her to regard the locum with annoyance and scepticism. First, the absent partners were going to a travel health conference in Mexico to present a paper which she co-wrote with them, but the sponsoring pharmaceutical company would only pay for doctors to attend. Secondly, the last locum the practice employed had been pompous beyond belief (in Totty's opinion) and strutted around the practice as if he owned the place. Finally, and this got to Totty more than anything, particularly given Dr Manley's attitude, he had asked the senior partner who recommended him if it would be all right for him to get some experience in pelvic examination and the taking of cervical smears. It had been agreed that the locum could improve his skills with patients who had a clinical need, and that Totty would help him with this as she was the most experienced practice nurse.

Totty chatted to Dr Manley over a lunch-time sandwich, and found herself thinking that she quite liked him. The afternoon clinic came before either nurse or doctor could get to know each other better. As usual, Totty and the other practice nurse saw patients on their own; these women generally just needed advice, routine assessment and cervical smears. If anything more complicated was needed, the nurse involved the GPs. One such case was a patient named Ann Wai, who was seeing Totty. A couple of months ago Ann had had a polyp removed from the wall of her vagina, and she was now attending for a check to see that everything was all right, in addition to having a routine smear. After informing the patient that the doctor was to conduct an internal examination and take the smear, and explaining how this would proceed, Totty filled Dr Manley in with the details of Ms Wai's history, and asked him into the treatment room.

The practice nurse stood slightly behind her patient, holding her hand as she lay on the examination couch, as Dr Manley began the procedure. Totty thought how uncomfortable and potentially distressing it must be for a woman to be examined in this way, and she really felt that she was needed to console her patient. She was irritated in that this was the main reason for her going out of her way to attend a Marie Curie course at her own expense and become competent in taking smears. What with four male GPs this was the least she could do for patients. 'Now we have taken a step back just so that Manley here can get up to speed with something he doesn't really need to do anyway,' Totty thought to herself. Totty held Ann's hand gently, but she felt her attention drift off for a couple of minutes as she concentrated on someone she could just see through the window blind making a real hotchpotch of parking outside the practice. Suddenly, Totty's attention snapped back to the treatment room. She thought that Dr Manley was having a problem and looked up to see if he was all right. The doctor's face was contorted as if he was in pain, and Ann Wai clearly winced — she was in pain. Totty leaned over and held the locum's hand, helping him guide the speculum in place. Things didn't get much better as David Manley poked a wooden spatula backwards and forwards as if he was playing a game of miniature snooker (Totty's thoughts). Once he had 'taken' the smear, the doctor then left it on the couch between Ann's legs, and calmly said 'There you are nurse, sort that for me will you?' and with that, he promptly left the room.

Totty Maize looked at the slide, apologised to Ann, and within seconds took another spatula for a further smear, which she correctly applied to a slide. Dr Manley's attempt was relegated into the sharps box. Totty stayed with her patient and helped her to dress before bidding her goodbye. She then sat in the treatment room for a few minutes, thoughts ranging from irritation to anger racing across her mind. She eventually jumped up and having checked that no patients were with the locum, stormed in with the exclamation 'what the hell do you think you were playing at?'

## Outcome

At first, Dr Manley was calm and collected. 'What do you mean nurse?' or something like that, was his reply, so Totty recalled later. She calmed a little: 'Well, look, shall I tell you where you went wrong then?' But as Totty went on to explain how to insert a speculum and take a smear properly, Dr Manley retorted: 'I think I did rather well actually. I really can't see what the fuss is about. I can see why that is a nursy thing now; you don't need to be a doctor to do it, do you now.' Thoughts of the hours spent in the classroom and practical experience undertaken flashed through Totty's memory: 'The arrogant ...' 'Look here. Dr Sorrenson asked me to help you improve your technique. It is obvious it needs improving, so let me help,' Totty persisted. 'Nurse, dear' (Totty winced), 'I don't think you are in a position to judge my medical skills, do you? As a matter of fact, I think I will be just fine taking all the smears for the rest of my time here. Now, I must get on.' With this, David Manley gestured for Totty to leave the room. Turning rather purple, she did just that.

Still irritated, Totty told her practice nurse colleague, Cindy, what had happened. 'Are you sure he was that bad Totty? I mean, come on — you had it in for him from the start didn't you?' As tears streamed down Totty's face, it was all too apparent to Cindy that Totty was sure he was. 'That arrogant *** couldn't care less about our patients; he's just got something to prove. I can't let him carry on like that.' The nurses didn't know what to do next. They were unsure whether to tell the other doctors about their concerns; one of them actually knew the locum, or so they thought. They decided to ring their professional organisation for guidance, in this instance the RCN.

After much discussion, it was resolved that Totty, with the support of Cindy, should tell the senior of the GPs remaining in the practice exactly what had happened, and ask that some action be taken. Unfortunately, the GP concerned was extremely sceptical, and said that Totty was blowing things out of proportion, after all she had admitted to being distracted and had been looking out of the window, hadn't she?

The nurses lost confidence in their GP colleagues, and rang for further guidance. One more go at Dr Manley was suggested. This time, though, the Doctor got extremely angry with Totty and was shouting so loudly that she really thought he was going to hit her if she didn't back down and leave his room. The next step was for the nurses to speak to the practice nurse facilitator at the FHSA. She was well known to the RCN, and would take them seriously. The nurse adviser did indeed take them seriously; in fact she arrived at the practice within 30 minutes of Totty's phone call. She had Totty write down everything she could remember of Dr Manley's interaction with Ann Wai, and subsequent incidents. She took the statement from Totty, assured the nurses that they had done the right thing, and said she would take it back to the FHSA.

Once back at the FHSA, the nurse adviser located her GP colleague, in order to discuss the best way of dealing with the incident. The response from the GP adviser was, however, very similar to that of the GP in Totty's practice, i.e. disbelief and a hint that the nurse must have been imagining it. After all, if Dr Sorrenson had recommended the locum he must be satisfactory.

It was now the nurse adviser's turn to call the RCN for advice. Fortunately, I had recently been on the same working party as the secretary for the local medical committee (LMC) of this area, and a phone call to her was obviously in order. Within an hour, representatives of the LMC had met with Dr Manley, and after he berated them just as he had Totty Maize, they 'arranged' for the FHSA to have him replaced.

# Discussion

As we considered earlier in Chapter 3, practice nurses are required to comply with their *Code of Professional Conduct*, especially clause 11 which requires them to:

> *'...report to an appropriate person or authority, having regard to the physical, psychological and social effects on patients and clients, any circumstances in the environment of care which could jeopardise standards of practice;'*

When combined with clause 2 which required Totty Maize to ensure that no omission on her part or within her sphere of responsibility was detrimental to the interests of patients, and the overriding clause 1 that she must always act in the interests of patients, there was no option but to bring forward her testimony about the action of Dr Manley.

In the practice situation, it was reasonable to assume that the senior partner in the practice was 'an appropriate person or authority', and the reluctance to take the nurse seriously was to be condemned. The next logical step was to speak with the nurse adviser at the FHSA. If Totty had not taken these steps, she would have been in breach of her *Code* and would have failed in her accountability to her patient and her profession.

The lack of support the practice nurses and nurse adviser received from medical colleagues at the FHSA was inexcusable. They were giving evidence of a clear example of bad practice but were not taken seriously. Dr Manley's assertion that a practice nurse was not in a position to judge his medical competency could well have held up in another situation, but Totty was an expert practitioner so far as taking smears was concerned, and was clearly in a position to judge his ability. At least when Dr Sorrenson heard what had happened on his return, he offered his profuse apologies to Totty, and took both Cindy and herself out for a good dinner. It would take more than a dinner date to persuade Totty to forgive David Manley, but she was pleased to have the team she knew and worked well with back together again.

My colleagues from the LMC assured me that Dr Manley would be dealt with appropriately. I made sure they understood that the nurses could well have taken the decision to report him to the General Medical Council, but felt so weary of the situation that they were happy enough that any potential harm had been removed from their patients.

In summary, the *Code of Professional Conduct* requires a great deal from nurses, but that is a hallmark of a profession, and Totty's response to its requirements was the essence of accountability. While individual practitioners are responsible for their actions, they do deserve the support of colleagues when they have been courageous enough to speak up in the interest of patients.

# Further reading

Cole A (1993) Whistling in the wind? (Staff still have fears about whistleblowing). *Nursing Times* **89**(26): 20

Howard G (1994) Whistleblowers: new legal protections, (Under the Trade Union Reform and Employment Rights Act 1993). *Occupational Health* **46**(3): 95–6

Kiely MA, Kiely DC (1987) Whistleblowing: disclosure and its consequences for the professional nurse and management. *Nursing Management* **18**(5): 41-42; 44–5

Lennane KJ (1993) 'Whistleblowing': a health issue, (Response of organisations to whistleblowing and the effects on individuals involved). *Br Med J* **307**: 667–70

Smith R (1989) Profile of GMC: dealing with sickness and incompetence: success and failure. *Br Med J* **298**: 1695–8

Tadd V (1994) Professional codes: an exercise in tokenism? (Effectiveness of the UKKC's code of Professional conduct in empowering nurses and supporting whistleblowers). *Nursing Ethics* **1**(1): 15–23

Wright S (1992) The case for confidentiality, (Legal aspects for nurses who whistleblow). *Nursing Standard* **6**(14): 52–3